The Christian State of Life

ADRIENNE VON SPEYR

The Christian State
Of Life

Edited by Hans Urs von Balthasar

TRANSLATED BY
SISTER MARY FRANCES McCARTHY

IGNATIUS PRESS   SAN FRANCISCO

Title of the German original:
Christlicher Stand
© 1956 Johannes Verlag
Einsiedeln, Switzerland

Cover by Victoria Hoke Lane

Contents

The Christian State of Life

I

Preparation

The Lord's Choice

Children who live in Christian surroundings usually adapt themselves imperceptibly and without much ado to the forms of Christian life. Not until later in life do they discover the inner content of these forms. While the child is still young, while the words are still strange and the sentences meaningless to him, his mother begins to pray simple prayers with him. At some point, the child begins to ask questions about what he is doing. He begins to understand. Prayer is no longer just something he does with his mother; slowly but surely it comes to be a conversation with God. The form reveals the meaning that lies beneath it. Or it can happen, at Sunday school or elsewhere, that the child encounters expressions he does not understand, and his mother explains their meaning to him. When this happens, the child proceeds from the content of a prayer to its form.

If the child's religious instruction is a good one, the face of the Lord shines forth more and more clearly from the form and content of every prayer. The child understands that he has been enrolled in a service that is required of all Christians and that was first offered to the Father by Jesus Christ. All the child's previous experiences direct his attention to the Lord: prayer, visits to church, the attitude of those praying around him, conversations with adults, everything that takes place in a religious atmosphere. Perhaps the angels played an important role in his childhood experience: he has been told that he has a guardian angel and that the other children have one, too. But angels are servants of the Lord. Or he has become aware of evil and has been told that evil caused the Lord's death. The things he learns—to join his hands in prayer, to genuflect, to be quiet in church—are things he must do to please the Lord. Eventually he forms a mental picture of the Lord and understands that the Lord did everything to please his Father. The Lord's words and deeds, his attitude of obedience, his death on the Cross—all these were acts of service to the Father. The Son's whole life can be summarized in one word: *choice*. He chose to serve the Father.

At such a moment, the child may perhaps comprehend that everything in his life thus far that has had to do with God is meaningful only in relation to the Son's choice. What he has hitherto regarded merely as custom, ceremony or inclination will henceforth determine the course his life will take, just as the Lord's choice determined the course of his life. The Son fulfills a mission; he lives for the sake of the task assigned to him. But he does nothing for himself. On the contrary, he does everything with and for the Father. Everything leads back to the divine unity from which the Son proceeds and from which he was never separated during his life on earth.

It may be that the child will begin now to ponder in his soul the possibility of entering the Lord's service. The Son did not make his choice so that he could travel a way reserved for him alone. By the very act of traveling it, he opened to persons of faith the possibility of making the same choice. Is it possible that my life, too, is being directed along this way? School, recreation, conversations at home and with friends, plans for the future, present inclinations and disinclinations: could all these things be brought into a unity that is related to the Lord's choice? It is not necessary to call the individual elements into question but only to bring them into order. None of them need be lost, but each of them must be given an ultimate meaning.

The Choice of One Called by God

Does such a possibility exist? How does it make itself known? Perhaps the child is still too young to envision a practicable path. Or perhaps he has a vague intimation of the way he is to go, but the concept is clouded by the weaknesses and uncertainties of youth. Perhaps he does not himself quite believe that it can be realized; or, if he does believe it, if he seriously regards himself as one with a choice to make, he does not see how he can make it. He is still too immature to make a choice that will affect his whole future. Perhaps the most he can do is leave the matter open, steadfastly refrain from making any choice at this time, decide nothing in haste. In this way, his life becomes a kind of study—not of himself but of what is being offered him. He tries to deepen the experiences he has already had, to study the interrelationships of things around him, until he truly understands them and can assimilate and order them. In doing so he becomes more and more aware that there is no such thing as chance, that what seems to have been offered him by chance is actually full of meaning and that this meaning is not an isolated one, not a passing phenomenon, but a part of that interrelationship of phenomena whose total meaning is not yet apparent to man, although it exists in God. The proper choice for one who has not yet reached maturity is to hold himself in readiness for the choice that is still hidden in God. That is not to say that he may not have a distinct preference for certain subjects or kinds of work. But he will never regard the things he pursues and loves and desires for himself as final choices. He will know that they are parts of a whole that rests in God. Yet this fact will not prevent him from devoting himself wholeheartedly to the tasks that lie before him. On the contrary, he will surrender himself wholly to the work that is clearly presented to him in the here-and-now. He may take pleasure in it, but he must not regard it as an ultimate choice. His devotion must have the potential of reaching beyond its present horizon, and it must somehow suggest the existence of this greater potentiality in the background of the limited object to which it is presently referred. It is not important that he cannot picture to himself this wider horizon. It need not—and does not—matter that everything is provisional. He knows that he is still growing toward maturity and must undergo a constant and rapid succession of new experiences, in the process relinquishing the narrower concepts of childhood. What he is doing now will not receive its final, conclusive meaning until later in any case. While he is growing, his principal concern must be to remain free—that is, to be always at God's disposal. For this reason, he will avoid whatever can limit him spiritually, whatever seems to be without purpose, whatever does not in some way open him and lead him to the Lord.

The Choice Made by Others

When a young person experiences again and again, particularly in prayer, that the Lord has a plan for him, and when he perceives this experience as an admonition to hold himself in readiness for whatever the Lord may ask him to do, he becomes more and more aware of the distance that separates him from the Lord. The choice lies with the Lord; it does not yet lie in the young person's soul. At some point, there arises in him a certainty that he will someday have the strength to make a definitive choice. But such an action requires time and reflection. He begins to approach the matter by observing the people around him. He tries to look into the souls of his youthful companions to see if, by any chance, they are moved as he is moved. It may be that his conversations with them will awaken in them the thought of a choice that is possible and required. At home, among his brothers and sisters, among all those with whom he comes into contact, he will raise the question more and more explicitly. It may be that he will have few opportunities to discuss it and must therefore rely more often than not on such norms as are likely to suggest themselves to one of his age. He will study his acquaintances to see if they, too, experience the separation from God that he experiences, if it is an important issue in their lives and if they have made any effort to come closer to the Lord. And because, in the short time at his disposal, he is not able to speak with many persons, because he lacks the maturity to assess the interior development of those around him or the process by which they have become what they are, he will be greatly troubled; he will feel perhaps more than he should that people have, for the most part, been too little concerned about the matter, that they have not only failed to choose but are so accustomed to not choosing that they know no other way of acting. They have, as it were, withdrawn into a shell that not only protects them from but also cuts them off from and constantly deadens them to both God and the world. They are no longer aware of the urgency of the question that absorbs the young person. He, in his turn, is alienated by their attitude, for he is about to undertake something that will effectively cut him off from those who have cut themselves off. Perhaps it has been his privilege to meet individuals who have preserved their openness and the breadth of their horizons, who are obviously continually striving to be the servants of the Lord or at least of a Christian idea—to provide some genuine service in an area that justifies their total commitment. These are individuals who see not only what is close to them but also what is far off and who reserve the right to commit themselves even more fully should circumstances require it. But such individuals will always be the exception. Most people draw their horizons in upon themselves. They want to look, as it were, at the high cliffs, not at the distant plains—not at what lies behind the obstacles they themselves have raised. Without doubt, alienation and resignation are the two attitudes the young person will encounter most frequently as he looks inquiringly about him.

If he is fortunate enough to have grown up in a truly Christian family, the choice made by his parents will have a positive value in his eyes; the generation gap will not destroy his feeling of sharing a common service with them. But he will also be aware that his service, or at least the way in which he will accomplish it, may be quite different from theirs, although both they and he are serving the same Lord. He will be particularly interested in the choice made by the priests he may know, whether diocesan priests or members of a religious order. He will be able to sense whether their decision was made entirely in the light of their desire to serve and whether they have consecrated their lives and all their powers to the Lord. He will observe them with the critical eye of youth and with a particular intensity of concentration. He will expect them, if their choice was a genuine one, to live in a detachment from the world that does not alienate them from life but rather imprints on their existence a mark of special distinction. They ought to be happier, more cheerful and composed, more sensible and wise than other people. There ought to be a glow about them that proclaims immediately that the service of the Lord is something right and proper for man, something that bestows upon him the peace that surpasses understanding. In his brief encounters with them, the young person will be attentive to discover how the signs and effects of their choice are manifest in the way in which they give themselves, in the words of their homilies, in their whole attitude. It may well be that they are objects of his curiosity rather than of his understanding; yet this curiosity will have its source not only in self-centeredness but also in a genuine striving to find what belongs to the Lord. Later he will direct his attention also to the Church herself as distinct from the person of the priest: perhaps to a general impression of the Mass as an event; to the design and arrangement of the interior of a church; to the homily and its content, quite apart from the priest who delivers it; to the traditional form of devotional exercises; to the conduct of the congregation; to Christian customs;

to the Church's presence at and consecration of the significant events of life; to everything that the Church's existence can offer and that man can expect of her. He will consider all these things in the light of the fundamental Christian choice, the choice of the people of the Lord to serve him. He will compare the atmosphere of the Church with that of his worldly surroundings, will weigh imponderables against imponderables in an attempt to discover if what the Church is offering is capable of spurring him on toward a definite choice, if it lights his way thereto, if it offers him a guarantee that, once he has made his choice, the Church will accompany and support him.

It will not be easy for him to study the Church thus objectively, for he does not have the necessary knowledge to do so. He will be confronted by an abundance of manifestations and will know that they all point toward a center, just as the individual utterances of the Lord, taken together, are the expression of his nature as Word of the Father. But it will be difficult for him to regard as parts of an indivisible unity both those things that he loves and that are meaningful to him and those that are repugnant to him and that he may, in some instances, even reject. He would like to pick and choose, to be reassured on certain points, so that he can rest secure in what pleases him and can turn his face to the things that suit him and his back to those that do not. Little by little, however, he will understand that he cannot make such a selection; the Church must always be accepted as a whole. He may be justly alienated by some things, but he cannot change them, cannot even deny that the things that alienate him belong to—contribute to—the Church's unity. Even if secularization has so distorted these things that their surface no longer reflects their true nature, he will come to realize that they are, at their roots, still what they were intended to be.

If he looks to his surroundings for guidelines in making his choice, he discovers not only that the world around him—lay persons, priests, Church—is constantly acquiring more meaning and more precise contours in this regard but also that he himself is changing and that his concept of what is important or not important, what is far or near, is altering. It is not just that he is growing and becoming more mature, gaining a broader perspective and the ability to make finer distinctions, but also that he is being affected by the nature of what he observes around him; what he is putting to the test is also relentlessly testing him and shifting the balances within him. Even as he considers, he is also to some extent being considered. He will gradually relinquish his earlier a priori attitude of standing apart from things, of seeing them as objects to be observed while himself remaining aloof from them; he will find himself in the midst of them, delivered over to them, influenced by them. His previous reflections about them will now be turned in upon himself, will lay hold of him and toss him back and forth among themselves in order to smooth his edges. Unsuspected vistas will open up even in his own inmost being. Where he thought he had only an external battle to wage, he will discover that he has become immersed in the battle and that he is being judged even as he judges.

All these things will change his attitude. If he has thus far been eclectic in his attitude toward the experiences of life and unwilling to commit himself to any of them, if he has been content to let things come to him as he stood unmoved and indifferent in the midst of them, he must now join the fray. He must confront the problems and issues that impinge violently upon him from every side. The service he had thought to render does not begin when he expected it to begin. He had expected it to begin *after* he had made his choice. Instead, he finds himself compelled to a service that begins even now, before that choice. His very hesitancy is a form of service, for it stands in the service of this service. Even as he tests the possibilities, he must allow himself to be tested by them. If he is sincere in doing so, there can be nothing better suited to open his eyes than this compulsion to let things take their course, to let himself be brought to his goal. And the more serious he has been from the beginning, the more serious will be the questions and the possibilities of choice that will now present themselves for his consideration.

***

If this tentative groping toward the choice of a way of life has the Lord for its goal—his nature, his service of the Father, his undeviating obedience—it will be accomplished in grace. It is impossible for one not prompted by grace to act in faith to make the Lord the center of his thoughts and plans. Contemplation of one's surroundings and of the Church, which is ultimately a contemplation of the effects of Christ's obedience in today's world, a contemplation that involves and acts upon and disturbs the tranquility of the one who contemplates, clearly demonstrates its character as grace. Every time someone in the world chooses, there shines forth a tiny light that has its source in the great central light that is the grace of Christ. To see these tiny lights and to evaluate them objectively, the observer must see them from the point of view of grace. He tries to make clear to his own faith the effect of faith upon the people around him and upon the Church. It is not difficult to do this while reading the Gospels or while engaged in prayer and contemplation, while directly concerned with the Person of the Lord; in such instances, he knows that he has been transported directly into the world of grace and has been touched by it. But he knows, too, that he cannot ignore the world and the Church and still expect to find the Lord. The Lord has established channels of grace in his Church, in those who have chosen him in faith and also in those who seek him.

It is at this point in his seeking that the young person realizes that he is not alone but is part of a vast multitude that is struggling as he is struggling to choose a way of life. However long he has waited for an answer that does not come, he has not, as he may often be tempted to think, become the victim of his search. He need not fear that he is wasting time. On the contrary, he may assume with confidence that everything will come to him under the guidance of grace—that the grace he seeks is seeking him. As a seeker after grace, he wanted to be objective and imagined that this meant he must be neutral, un-involved, colorless. But in the world of grace, what is objective is itself grace, for God's truth is one with his grace. That is why he who seeks to touch truth has already been touched by God's grace.

II

The Choice

The Channels of Choice

One who gives serious consideration to the choice he must make and spares no effort to make the right one will be shocked at the number of people who fail to choose. He will discover that many of the people around him lead a life of chance, taking life as it comes and accepting what it brings them with no reflection, no genuine attempt to come to terms with the life they live and, in consequence, no conscious and free acceptance of it. They are indifferent toward life, neither alienated from it nor truly united with it in total free fulfillment of themselves. They live as though life with its joys and sorrows were merely a fact of nature and one who lives it merely another such fact, a creature who must bow to fate and be grateful that he exists at all. Such a life is far removed from the gift of grace that the Creator intended for his free creatures and that the Lord makes available again to Christians. Grace awakens and sharpens in the Christian the sense of responsibility for his own existence.

For one who is still young, still groping toward his choice in prayer and contemplation, it is a great shock to discover the disparity in his world between grace and human indifference. He sees that it is possible to miss what is most important in life, and that this happens frequently. He sees also that living faith—faith in the possibility of free and serious choice—is absent wherever men live in stolid resignation. The discovery stirs him to action. The attitude of observer is something temporary that must lead to action, to choice. God grants him this time of indecision so that man may examine his choice in the light, so that all the alternatives emerge and so that he may realize the consequences of choosing and of not choosing. But his role as a more or less critical observer who summons all things before him in judgment is necessarily of short duration. Were he to continue in it too long instead of summoning the courage to make a choice, he would discover after a few short years that there was no longer any appreciable difference between himself and those who live their lives in passive resignation. What began in grace would end in weary indifference. His role as observer, the joy he took in the possibilities that shimmered before his eyes, his particular pleasure in contemplating them without committing himself to any of them—all these would lead inexorably to the loss of life and the drying up of its sources.

Once someone becomes aware that he has been an observer for long enough, this very observation will urge him toward the choice. At this point there are many ways open to him.

He can review in solitude and by his own efforts the various possibilities that lie before him: life in the married state, life outside the married state and, in the latter case, life in the priestly or religious state. Gradually, by persistent elimination of unsuitable options, he can arrive at what is, for him, the correct choice. If he is thinking of the religious life, he will familiarize himself with existing orders, congregations and other forms of religious life; he will try to learn more about them and to discover, by conversation with their members, by reading and by his own observations, to which of them he is best suited. In doing so, he will maintain an outward appearance of pronounced objectivity—all the more, perhaps, because, as one who is merely seeking information, he does not want to become an object of special attention or cultivation and is in fact afraid of being unduly influenced. And one day, on the basis of a tentative decision, he will present himself to the head of the community he wishes to join, asking for admittance and thereby for confirmation of his choice.

But this way is not without its disadvantages. It is better to discuss one's choice with an appropriate person than to conceal it from everyone. Failure to discuss it seems, indeed, to indicate a certain overestimation of one's own personality and a corresponding distrust of one's fellowmen—tendencies that will have to be overcome during one's religious life and that will be experienced as obstacles at the beginning of it. Such a way can only make the road to a choice more difficult, without guaranteeing any fruitfulness as a result. This does not mean that the essential fruitfulness of the evangelical life will thereby be threatened; it does mean, however, that the spontaneous fruitfulness that resides in a proper choice and in the road that leads to it might be obstructed. Anyone entering upon this way should be aware that there exists, for the world around him, a blessing of participation in his choice. Even if this world reacts with delays, objections or open resistance to the choice he will make, it may be struck and impressed by the certainty of the one choosing and by the grace that is apparent in that certainty. One who acts as if his choice concerned only God and himself and who is content to make inquiries without letting himself be counseled deprives the Church of a fruit.

A second way of making one's choice is the attitude of complete receptivity and self-surrender. He who makes the choice knows that he has been chosen even before he chooses; therefore the way before him has been determined and shaped by God, and the persons he meets on this way are not there by accident but have been placed there by God. Consequently, he will make himself known as a seeker, particularly to those who have been before him along the same path. This does not mean that he will expose himself indiscriminately to their influence or that he will transfer to them, at a first meeting, the responsibility for the decision he himself must make. It means rather that, within his relationship to God and in the mystery of the oneness of love of God and love of neighbor, he will affirm his relationship to his fellowmen, his fellow Christians, those who, like himself, are seeking to know the way they must go and those who have already made their choice; that he will open himself to them without fear, but only so that he can weigh the matter again—and again without fear—with God in prayer. He will neither fold in upon himself like a mimosa blossom nor yield irresolutely to persistent attempts at persuasion. Just as he has hitherto regarded his fellowmen as objects given him by God for his observation, so now, in a like attitude of openness and generosity, he will willingly let himself be observed by them.

There is also a third way open to him. When he feels that the time is ripe, he can set aside a certain time for making his choice. Perhaps he will look upon all he has observed up to this time as material to be reviewed in a few days of recollection before he makes his choice. Perhaps he will make his decision in the ecclesial context of a retreat that he will undertake in a state of interior detachment, taking with him what he has thus far experienced, but with a will to return and submit everything to God so that he may stand in his original state before him. He desires to abandon himself during these days of prayer and divine guidance to God's will, which he seeks to see and understand for himself in his contemplation of the Son, who fulfills it to perfection. It should be noted here that no one, whether in retreat or not, should make a decision that he does not intend to test by submitting it to the pressures of life in the world. Whoever has reached a decision during days of recollection must dare to return to the old life with all the joy or, as the case may be, all the burden of the choice he has made in order to find there the confirmation of his decision. This does not mean that he will now trust himself to everyone or let himself be swayed by everyone, but rather that he will let the bridge he has built be tested by the world's burdens.

There are, we might note, two ways of making a retreat. One way is for the retreatant to listen to the conferences, but at the same time hold himself aloof from the retreat master, assuming that he is cooperating sufficiently with the spirit of the retreat if he is open to what is being said. He regards prayer and all that concerns the choice he must make as intensely private matters—matters he must think through in complete isolation with God. But such isolation runs the risk of becoming isolation with oneself. The mystery of self is given precedence over the mystery of community. Above all, such a one forgets that the mystery is in reality God's mystery, and that God has purposely brought him to this retreat master—who, after all, is here to some extent as the result of his own choice.

It is more usual, therefore, for the retreatant to speak openly with the retreat master about the nature of the choice to be made and to accept with gratitude whatever advice he may be able to give. But the retreat master can advise only those who open their hearts to him in childlike confidence, showing him both the light and the darkness that is in them. In this advisor the retreatant will recognize the objectivity of the office instituted by the Lord. This does not mean that he will seek to lay upon the retreat master the burden of what must be ultimately his own decision, but that he will accept that advice, assimilate it and let it supplement his own views, which have perhaps been narrowed by his previous isolation or by other causes; that he will at least no longer regard his own judgment as the primary norm of his conduct or allow its limitations to acquire imperceptibly the character of immutability. A retreat offers one the opportunity of becoming a new person in a new spiritual environment, a person who has made his choice and has now only to test its strength in the old environment. Since the days of retreat and the special graces they offer are numbered, it would be a pity if one were to be at the end of them exactly as one was at the beginning: determined to put off the decision until some unspecified future. If nothing else, one should have arrived at a parting of the ways. A retreat sincerely undertaken for the purpose of choosing a state of life should, at the very least, produce in the retreatant a visible shift in the balance of his preferences.

***

In a retreat master, three qualities coincide. First, he presents the way of choice as something he has himself experienced; second, he is mindful that the retreat is the Church's objective way of helping those who are making a choice; third, he familiarizes himself with the personal problems that confront each of the retreatants. By the objectivity of his conferences, he seeks to make known equally to all the retreatants the possibilities and ways of choosing that are open to them. The Spiritual Exercises are, by their very nature and structure, designed to accomplish this goal. In addition, the retreat master has the opportunity of speaking personally with those who seek his guidance. In doing so, he must preserve all three of the qualities mentioned above: as one who has already made his choice, he has subjective experience that he must now incorporate into the objectivity of the retreat, without renouncing, in the process, his responsibility for the subjective situation of each retreatant. The retreatant expects of him both personal involvement in what he is experiencing and preservation of ecclesial objectivity. Only thus can the retreat master differentiate subjective and objective elements in the retreatant, but in individual cases he can only be certain of what is objective when what is subjective has been clearly outlined. He is not dealing with a purely objective entity, and therefore he cannot dwell upon general, abstract teachings; through insight into the subject, he

must come as close as he can to the objective truth that
applies to that subject. This is because of the statements—
always more or less subjective—of the retreatant, who is
attempting to present himself as he is. Only very seldom
does the objective truth present itself clearly from the
outset; usually some subjective husks must be peeled off,
and then begins a kind of weighing. In the process as
much as possible of what is objective must be laid bare,
and in such a fashion that both the retreatant and the
retreat master recognize it as objective. Perhaps the
two of them have approached the question with very
different standards of measurement, wishes and considerations; the only thing that binds them is the impartial
wish that the objective divine will be fulfilled.

The Lord also dealt differently with each of his disciples. He drew them into his actual service and spoke to
them in a way that was right for each of them. Nor can
we doubt that he also took into account the situation
of each individual. And as he invited them, so they
responded. From this we may deduce the great responsibility of the retreat master, who points the way to
the Lord and is his official representative, not only when
he holds conferences and dispenses the sacraments, but
even more especially when he speaks with a retreatant
in private.

To achieve clarity, the retreat master must know why
each retreatant is making the retreat and what considerations led him to do so precisely at this time. In this way
he can discern the core of the retreatant's expectations
and judge the rightness or wrongness of his motives.
Even if the retreatant fails to make a choice at this time,
the retreat master can do much to prepare the way for
future efforts.

***

During the Spiritual Exercises, the young retreatant views his previous existence, his environment and perhaps even his own experiences in a situation remote from his everyday routine. The remoteness is increased above all by the fact that he is learning to view these things from the perspective of prayer and is not exposed to the small irritations of daily living. He has distanced himself from his customary environment. Perhaps he becomes aware that he has failed in some essential respects, that he has been lacking in decisiveness; he realizes what things he has allowed to fetter him, what is wrong with his view of the world, where his sins have necessitated byways and detours that he only now recognizes for what they actually are. There is, perhaps, much in his relationship with the people around him that he regarded as fixed as long as he was still among them but which he now perceives as in need of correction. He sees what he might have been able to avoid or accomplish by a word here, a greater decisiveness there. From the perspective of his present detachment, his whole relationship to his neighbor takes on a new aspect. He makes various resolutions regarding it. But he runs the risk of falling back into the old errors once he has returned to his customary routine. Yet, because the light of the Spiritual Exercises is so objective and brings him so close to God, he ought to do his utmost to see that it produces at least some lasting fruit. If he returns from retreat with new resolutions and even with a decision about his state of life, that fact will certainly not remain hidden. If his decision should refer to the priesthood or the religious life but cannot at once be translated into action, it will nevertheless bear noticeable fruit in the meantime. For a brief time he will continue to live with his family and in the old surroundings, and he will have an opportunity to influence others that will be all the more significant because it will not occur again. It should be taken seriously: not in such a way that the decision he has made will be endangered by his "making use" of his time in the world, but in such a way that he will be strengthened in his decision and will also seek, by his attitude, to make it as comprehensible as possible to those around him.

Where there is a question of a decision about one's state of life, the people around one will also want to be heard. But since they generally have little insight into the matter, their contributions are often without importance or sense. Some of them are blindly "for" the decision because they see in it some advantage for themselves; others are just as blindly "against" it because they have no concept of what a vocation entails and are daunted by the unexpected. Nevertheless, each of them feels impelled to voice his opinion. The young person should listen to their words but should regard them as words to be confronted with the word of God. Often enough, they are empty words, but he can sow a seed in them. It would be unwise for the young person simply to ignore every objection and to move inexorably toward his goal without regard for the opinions of family or friends. Later, he will meet the same lack of understanding from other sources; hence he may regard the present situation as a training ground for his later traffic with men. He must learn to be firm without seeming to reject those whose views oppose his own; he must make an effort to help them understand his decision to the extent that it can be understood. Perhaps they will thus acquire some appreciation of the Christian vocation as such, not just of his own; perhaps some ties to the Church and between him and his family will be renewed and strengthened and made permanent. All the people close to him should receive as much grace as possible from his vocation and should feel as encouraged as possible in their faith and in their readiness to serve. If he is called to dedicate his whole being to the Lord, he cannot postpone this action until the day of his entrance into the novitiate or seminary. He must begin at once. He must seek to approximate in his life the life of Jesus of Nazareth. Where he once sought to discover how others made their decision, he must now, by his steadfastness and peace and by his inner joy, let his own decision come to fruition within him—and perhaps, in the process, help others who are called to serve the Lord to accept their vocations and so obviate many misunderstandings and prejudices. He can bring everyone around him one small step closer to God. But he will never forget that his own decision has already been made and will run its course at its own tempo. In the meantime, he must not be idle. He must put his affairs in order and make himself ready. If necessary, he must wait but under no circumstances waste his time or, through his own fault, prolong the period of waiting.

The Characteristics of the Choice

Once the moment of choosing has arrived, the concept of "choice" acquires, for him who chooses, an absolute and intimate vitality. It is not for him a question of something theoretical, but primarily of something practical, something that will determine the meaning of his whole life. It must be for him, therefore, a matter of the greatest urgency, of an inexorability that can be neither gainsaid nor ignored, of an intensity that does not allow him to water down the choice he must make or to continue weighing it until the "danger" has passed and nothing has happened. He must be as clear as possible in his own mind that God demands a choice of him now. Everything in his past life has been oriented toward this choice. Even though he lets the possibilities pass before him in quick succession, it is no longer distant eventualities that he contemplates but possibilities that affect his existence in the here-and-now, from which he must make his choice. And the choice is the outcome, not of a more or less hazardous game of chance, but of prayer before God. It is not what he had imagined or hoped it would be; it is God's clear demand on him here and now, where he is.

He has lived until now, but what he once was is now finished. It lies behind him. He has made some effort to shape it, but for the most part he has accepted it and let it take its course. The result has been a sum of experiences and efforts that, taken together, have prepared the way for what is to come, for what will give his life its definitive form and orientation. This must be brought about by God. That is true even if he who makes the choice is destined thereby to continue his life in the world. Even in such a case, it must be a new life, a life in which he completely accepts his responsibility before God. The time of letting himself be tossed by every wind must be brought firmly to an end and granted no extension.

Through the Spiritual Exercises, one who has a choice to make is given a clear introduction to the various states of life within the Church: the married state, the priest-hood, the religious state. That is the prerequisite of any genuine choice. But in the process of this clear intro-duction, the retreatant cannot impress upon himself too deeply that the point of all this is his own existence before God. He sees what is set before him, but he does not select, as he might select in a department store, what is most pleasing to himself; he must turn his gaze on God and what God is demanding of him. He must seek to understand where God wants him to be and must see whether he has the inner freedom to bend his own will to this will of God.

***

A person may begin the Spiritual Exercises with a firm purpose of making a choice at the end of them. He is certain that God will help him and will make his will known to him. For his part, he is determined to make his choice in such a way that it finds its meaning in God, giving to the life he has received from God a meaning that remains in God. The decision he will make during the Spiritual Exercises will be the fruit of his whole previous life: the "choice of choice" under the influence of prayer and with the will to be born again in grace to a life that will serve God in whatever place and whatever way may be pleasing to him.

But this service should also be the expression of the talents of the one serving. It is not permitted him to dispose of his life in a moment of enthusiasm as though he were possessed of no special qualities. He is responsible before God for the particular being that he is. The more strongly he keeps in mind what God has made him to be, the more wholly he gives himself to God, the more open he is to his retreat master, the more he desires to devote himself, with the Son, to the accomplishment of God's will, the more he will feel drawn to the *state of the evangelical counsels*. To live with the Lord as the Apostles did in a visible community, a community of obedience to him, an apostolate of the greatest possible breadth and freedom—whether it be an apostolate exclusively of prayer and contemplation or an apostolate in which contemplation and action are combined—this must appear as the ideal to the retreatant. Indeed, the emphasis on a life of total discipleship is inseparable from the Spiritual Exercises in their actual intention.[1] Nevertheless, it would be improper for the retreat master to try to persuade the retreatant to choose the evangelical state; he can only help him to make the right choice, the one offered to him by God. It is admittedly difficult to say with any degree of certainty how often the Exercises are conducted by the retreat master, and followed by the retreatant, as objectively as they should be. What can be said with certainty is that the number of vocations to the immediate following of Christ would be far greater if everyone could have the opportunity of making the Spiritual Exercises properly during his time of choice. It is not sufficient for the retreatant to awaken in himself a readiness to renounce all things and to draw as close as possible to the Cross of Christ. He who chooses must likewise consider whether he has the capabilities neces-

---

[1] It is my belief that the Lord, at the beginning of his public life when he began to call his Apostles, intended to let the call grow like a rolling snowball so that it would have been impossible to determine in advance how many of those addressed by him and called to conversion would, in the end, have chosen to become his immediate

sary for perseverance in the way he has chosen: the health, the spiritual gifts, the inner alertness that will keep him from drying up and withering so that no more living fruit can be expected of him.

Once he has seen his way clearly in prayer, he may no longer require the encouragement of the retreat master; he is ready to make known his decision. Under no circumstances, however, may he regard his calling by God as an event that has now happily taken place and leave all the rest more or less to chance. There is nothing more disastrous than a decision that has been made but not executed. The danger is great that he who hesitates, postpones and wavers about the choice he has made will come to regard it as a product of his imagination or even of a moment's unconsidered enthusiasm. The will to do what one has decided to do and the actual doing of it must be contained in the decision itself. If not, the retreatant will return to his earlier way of life in a worse state than if he had never made the Spiritual Exercises.

There are always those who enter upon the Spiritual Exercises with every evidence of a genuine good will in which they are later unable to persevere. It is quite

---

followers in the sense of the evangelical counsels. It is not inconceivable that Christian marriage has acquired, at the present time, a more positive meaning in relation to the kingdom of God than it would have had in primitive Christianity, where marriage was definitely seen as a concession. This does not mean that it was, for that reason, condemned. Most of the Apostles were married when the Lord first met them, but there is no mention of a marriage entered into by an Apostle after that meeting. Nevertheless, the Lord blessed the marriage at Cana, and he and his Mother were so well known and so well received there that he did not hesitate to attend the wedding feast with his disciples.

probable that they have a true desire to follow Christ. But, as soon as they return to the world, the experiences of the retreat are engulfed and insulated by the routine of their daily lives. They are grateful for what they have experienced and happy to have been raised even once to such an "ideal" level; the retreat has for them in retrospect the quality of a special event. On the other hand, it is never advisable for a retreatant to enter religious life immediately after completing the Spiritual Exercises. For that very reason, his choice must be so well grounded during the days of retreat that he feels absolutely and seriously bound by it—feels himself to be inwardly, even if not yet outwardly, in the state of life he has chosen.

The second possibility is the *secular priesthood*. Just as two elements were united in the Lord's calling of his Apostles—the call to personal discipleship and the call to an apostolic, ecclesial and hierarchic ministry—so in every vocation to the secular priesthood the first element, which establishes a link with the life of the evangelical counsels, will not be absent. But it will not be the dominant element. Or, at least, its nature will be, from the beginning, determined, if not actually circumscribed, by the second element: the study of theology, the administration of a parish, the dispensing of the sacraments, the ministry of education, the preaching, the pastoral interaction with one's neighbors. These and other similarly concrete duties stand before the eyes of one called to the secular priesthood, whereas one called to the evangelical counsels sees before him little or nothing that is concrete, but initially only the open path of discipleship. One who chooses the secular priesthood perceives the urgency of the Lord's precept "to leave all things" in a different way: he has and will continue to have deeper roots in family and community; he sees a certain value in the possession of what is useful and serviceable. He is more concerned with the Church's mission and with particular activities within the Church than with contemplation, especially with pure contemplation as it is practiced in the religious orders founded for that purpose. And in those orders in which contemplation is combined with action he sees, perhaps, too little of the personal freedom that would be his in greater measure in the secular priesthood. One who enters the religious life does so with no predetermined aims; he leaves everything open so that he can later be more easily assigned to a specific mission. The secular priest, on the other hand, reserves to himself from the beginning a certain freedom that he will not later be called upon to relinquish. Often, moreover, it is one particular aspect of the priestly life—the study of theology, perhaps, or religious instruction or the celebration of Holy Mass with the congregation—that especially attracts an individual and enables him later to bear with equanimity the other, less attractive, aspects. However that may be, his choice must also be accompanied by a genuine adherence to the counsels of Jesus and by a genuine will to personal discipleship. Accordingly, he must begin immediately after the Spiritual Exercises to live a life of personal discipleship, even if he is obliged, for one reason or another, to postpone his entrance into the seminary.

Something similar may be said also of the third possibility, that of the *married state*. No one who has once made the decision to marry should revert to a kind of bachelor existence, living his life inwardly and outwardly as though no such decision had been made. His decision must be put into execution. One who intends to marry must be serious, even before the marriage, about the demands he intends to place both upon himself and upon his wife. He must be sure that he has acquired all the spiritual building blocks for the structure he is planning: the education, the occupation and the wife as well. He must choose the way of life that will enable him to choose his wife wisely. He should not associate exclusively with male companions, nor should he live alone or away from his fellowmen except for those occasions when he requires their services. He will have a variety of motives for his choice: negative ones, in that he cannot imagine himself under the yoke of obedience or in the loneliness of a celibate life; positive ones, in that he regards it as a duty to live in freedom among free Christians in a community of marriage from which new, living impulses continually proceed.

It is inconceivable that the Spiritual Exercises should lead to a decision that has as its goal an egotistic plan of life. If the decision has been made in faith, it cannot fail to lead to a life of faith and of the apostolate. On the other hand, if the individual has decided in advance that he will continue in his present routine and live solely for himself, he might as well spare himself and the retreat master the effort of the retreat. There are some people who make a retreat for no other purpose than to experience some spiritual excitement and who, on the basis of what they experience, then try to dissuade others from making a retreat by parading before them, as an ultimate judgment on the Spiritual Exercises, their own failure to reach a decision or to choose a way of life. After the Spiritual Exercises, they are more closed and less fruitful for themselves and the people around them than they were before. They lacked the honesty to enter with open souls into the process that would have made their meeting with the Lord a vital one. And so they are inevitably disappointed by their experience and can pass on nothing but their disappointment. On the other hand, if they were actually moved by it, however slightly, and if they let themselves be raised by it, however briefly, from their preoccupation with earthly things but lacked the courage to reach a firm decision, they will later compensate for their failure by making this "sin of their youth" the object of their bitter and haughty scorn.

The Effects of the Call

A choice rightly made produces a change in the whole attitude of the one who makes it. It touches upon his relationship to God, to the people around him and to himself.

Toward *God* he experiences the gratitude of one who has been privileged to meet God and be guided by him and who is now aware that he must not forfeit the grace he has received. He is bound to God anew, not only in prayer; he tries, in all the relationships of his life, to respond adequately to the new claims upon him and to grow in his understanding of them. As a result of his choice, God reveals the Christian life to him in much more brilliant colors. He must so absorb this life that his whole being will henceforth be alert to what God is demanding of him; although he will never be able to meet these demands in their entirety, he will nevertheless be constantly aware of their significance. But his awareness must not be reserved solely for the demands of a later time; it is urgently needed precisely in the time immediately after the Spiritual Exercises, when the retreatant will have to start carrying out what he has planned. His every step must henceforth be taken in God and with the certainty of God's approval. He has a new commitment to God, a commitment that is enveloped in the grace so recently bestowed upon him and that is impossible of accomplishment without it.

There is also a change in his relationship to *the people around him*. As a result of his choice, his neighbors appear to him now in a new light. They have been entrusted to him anew, and he is to be increasingly at their disposal. Something of the new responsibility lies in his neighbors: they admonish him, challenge him and even, upon occasion, make him the object of new, exaggerated expectations. His fellowmen became his instructors at the moment when he began to understand the Christian life as an apostolic mission. Many of the people around him are, in fact, following the same path and feeling and bearing the same responsibility before God. From them he can learn how to cope with his own responsibility. Others are questioning, immature, helpless; he feels that he should have some answer for them, but as yet he has none. Thus the immaturity of some becomes a stimulus for his own maturation, which is the necessary condition of his giving any effective help.

Finally, there is a change in his relationship to *his own life*. It is no longer the existence of a self-seeking and unfolding ego but that of one who has been called by God, an existence that now becomes an objective service. His task is to help this objectivity to its full expression, to let appear in his life the mark of the vocation: that vocation which he has perceived before God and received from God's hands and that must be tested again and again before God in order to be right. In the existence of the one he has called, God must be able to recognize again, in the process of the former's being realized, the demand he placed on him. This thought can serve, in the future, as the foundation for his spiritual life and his entire attitude. In addition, there are the thousand and one steps that someone who has been called by God must take in order to achieve his end. If he has chosen the life of the evangelical counsels, he must decide on a particular religious community, must submit his application and must endeavor to satisfy the requirements of the order or congregation he has chosen. He must complete his studies, set his affairs in order, redeem his obligations, be interviewed. As far as possible, he must do all these things in the spirit of the order he has chosen, or of the priesthood if this has been his choice. If he marries, he must fulfill all the requirements and make all the arrangements before God, not separating the practical from the spiritual, but planning both with a unified awareness so that his choice will not be just an ideal floating above the earth but a thing of flesh and blood.

The Safeguards of the Choice

What has been won in the solitude of the Spiritual Exercises must be secured and strengthened in the time that follows. Of utmost importance in this regard is prayer, into which the themes of the Spiritual Exercises can be woven and which will help to keep the one who has chosen constantly mindful of the choice he has made. Also important is a clear awareness of what he has undertaken. The new way of life will not succeed just because it is better. It must be helped to succeed. One

must no longer expose himself unresisting to the influences of his environment. The new way of life may be
a search, but a search that must be powerful and in which
it has been promised that he who seeks will find. The
image of the Lord was so vivid during the Spiritual
Exercises because the whole atmosphere combined to
that end. This atmosphere is lacking after the Spiritual
Exercises, yet the image must be just as vivid. To
achieve this, one must have the courage to sacrifice
whatever militates against it: that lazy comfort with
which we constantly surround ourselves and that hinders
the quick and precise reaction of the soul. The light of the
gospel must shine everywhere unhindered.

   In truth, man's life is always a twofold one: on the one
side, his everyday life with its work and cares; on the
other, a life that interrupts his daily routine—a life of
holidays, travel, dreams, ideals and, for the Christian, of
prayer and meditation, to which belong also the days of
retreat. From our travels we return refreshed and filled
with colorful memories. But these memories do not
have the power to affect our attitude toward God or
toward the world around us. The journey to God, on the
other hand, must have a very different effect. If we have
met God sincerely, it should no longer be possible for us
to lose the reality of that meeting. For it pertains to God's
nature to be at least as real today as he was yesterday and
always. Hence we must approach with care the memory
of our meeting with him, for it is only figuratively and
accidentally a memory of something past. In the final
analysis, it is not only we who have interrupted our daily
routine during the days of the Spiritual Exercises. God,
too, has done so, for he has become real to us in a way he
has never done before. When we must return to our

everyday surroundings, we must do so in such a way that God continues to guide us. The choice we made during the Spiritual Exercises was perhaps the product of our cooperation with the grace of God; now, in the time of safeguarding it, it is almost a work of God against us. Our own participation has become more difficult; what stands forth now is the objectivity of the choice we have made, which now assumes primary importance and makes its claim upon us, somewhat like a child that has been brought into the world and must now be cared for. The one who makes the choice becomes less important than the choice he has made. It is no longer a question of safeguarding ourselves but of safeguarding the choice we have made, the will of God for us.

After the Choice

The time of the Spiritual Exercises is a time of reflection not only for the retreatant but also, to some extent, for those around him, who share his experience at a distance and who expect that he will be different after the Spiritual Exercises from what he was before them. They have even prepared for the change more or less; there has been a little gossip. Knowing this, one who returns after having made a retreat will, without ostentation or hypocrisy, try to exert a certain influence on those around him. This is all the more true in cases where the decision to make the Spiritual Exercises was greeted with reservations and often even with sarcasm by his family, who were convinced that he would be more or less the same after as before. Sometimes the fact that an individual makes the Spiritual Exercises is regarded by many as a sign of insincerity, while at the same time they worry lest he be unduly influenced thereby. Persons who are opposed in principle to the making of the Spiritual Exercises are usually those who no longer believe in an effectual intervention of grace. None of this is designed to make life easier for the one who has made the Spiritual Exercises but rather to increase his uncertainty. During the Exercises, he was perhaps like someone on a tightrope: he had to go forward quickly and surely, for he had no other way to go. Now the street is again as wide as it was before, yet he must walk as though it were narrow. In addition, he must let himself be tested by those around him and must do so without pretense, with the same honesty with which he had previously made his choice. As he was then transparent to God, so he must now be transparent to the people around him.

If the choice of a state of life was not made during the Spiritual Exercises, but rather in the course of everyday life, the accompanying circumstances are different. There is no external break either for the one who makes the choice or for those around him. In consequence, the discussion—perhaps the conflict—with other people will be less abrupt. Nevertheless, what is true for someone who made his choice during the Spiritual Exercises is also true for someone who did not: he must change after making his choice. He will not have to readjust himself to surroundings he has never left. The moment of choice will have and retain a certain solemnity for him, but this moment will be more closely linked to his everyday life than will that of one who made his choice during the Spiritual Exercises. Everything will be simpler and more hidden both in him and for the people around him.

III

Implementing the Choice

In Act

In the individual who has chosen, the choice must become an essential and living part of his existence. To this end it needs to be surrounded by care, just as the seed of a fruit, in order to remain alive, must be surrounded by the flesh of the fruit, which grows from the seed outward. Of the individual who has made his choice, certain actions are expected which proclaim his choice to the outside world. If he has chosen the religious life, for instance, he must see to the various formalities attendant upon his entrance. While he is busy with these external matters—to which he must turn his attention, for they have their own importance—the danger is never far distant that his decision will itself become externalized. He has given his life; the matter would seem to be closed and to require no repetition. Yet faith demands that this vocation, like every Christian vocation, continually emerge fresh and new from the original call, that it be generated anew in every action required by the call. Man's participation in God's call must be so linked to its source that it also embraces and accepts all the individual actions; that it not only bears externally and formally the impress of his vocation but also arouses in his soul the appropriate conviction and attitude before God: that

every exterior detachment, every renunciation of pos-
sessions or friends, every leave-taking from relatives,
home and family, must be matched by a corresponding
interior separation and preparation. Circumstances over
which the individual has some control play an important
part in the process of choosing: I want to be assigned to
this particular diocese, to follow this profession, to enter
this religious order. In pursuit of this goal I must write
this letter, take this trip, visit this prior or that superior.
And when these conditions have been met, I shall be
accepted. But there are also circumstances over which I
have no control. The first of these is myself, for I must
develop within the terms of my decision; I must find, in
all that happens, a meaning that will make me better able
to serve God. Also beyond my control are the pre-
requisites for the success of my plans: the results of tests
and the decisions of other persons with regard to me. For
it may be that, despite all my determination to give
myself entirely to God's service, I have reckoned with a
self that did exist when I made my choice but that no
longer perfectly perseveres. It may also happen that my
readiness to serve, my joy and my zeal suffer somewhat
because of my involvement in these formalities and other
external activities. The person to whom I must present
myself may be totally unappealing to me. He may point
out certain elements of the religious life that I had not
foreseen and that seem to me inessential. My task even
now is to consider and come to terms with the spirit of
the religious order I have chosen and with those of its
outward expressions that I do not yet comprehend. I
may not simply shake them off; I must affirm them. I
may not pass judgment on them but must receive them
lovingly. Thus there begins even now an emptying of

my own personality, which must nevertheless continue to exist at the locus of my decision and must be constantly regenerated from the concept of total service. This concept is so superpersonal that it can keep the personal element alive only by raising it to a higher level, into the service of the Lord. This is even now a training in that obedience to which I am not yet outwardly obliged, even though it exists, as obedience to the Lord, by virtue of my making the choice. If, on the other hand, I have chosen to enter the married state, then there will be many things in my preparation for marriage which, though I had not foreseen them, will show me aspects of my future married life that I must simply accept. I must accept my unappealing future mother-in-law, accustom myself perhaps to more cramped quarters than I was accustomed to at home, and so on. And I must do so, not superciliously as though I were basically too good for what is being asked of me, but in a genuine spirit of sympathy.

After the choice, there is always a danger that one will become too casual. Things will take their course, but my readiness is exhausted. I feel that my decision has "saved" me in God's sight, especially as long as "some action is being taken". To avoid this danger, one must regard the actions that lead to the final step as matters that concern one deeply—not just as the working out of an earlier decision but as the expression of a present frame of mind for which one is constantly seeking a more adequate expression. One must not let oneself be deceived. Many believe that once they have bestirred themselves to make the choice, they are exempt from further activity. But the carrying out of the choice must be undertaken, not in a sluggish spirit as though the moment of choice had been the high point of one's life, but rather in a growing awareness that regards every moment as a new beginning. It would be foolish, therefore, for one who has already made his choice to try to duplicate the enthusiasm and fervor that marked his prayer and his meeting with God at the time it was made. It is far more important that he heed the present will of God.

The flurry of the transition brings with it a multitude of activities that are externally meaningful and indispensable. But they must not be allowed to stifle the person's internal fullness, especially since the interval between choosing and attaining his goal is a unique and irrevocable epoch in his life, a legitimate interval with a meaning all its own. In looking back later, it will be meaningful to divide his life into the time before his choice of vocation, the time between the choice and the entrance into the chosen state, and the time after the entrance. The time of transition will reveal itself as a time of heightened activity which had, nonetheless, to preserve a contemplative relationship both to the call of God and to the vocation to which he was called. One called to enter the seminary or novitiate understands the world now in a way that will never again be possible for him. There is still time for him to retrieve lost opportunities, and the world still has a claim on him. He possesses a secret of Christian fruitfulness that is not intended for him alone but must be made manifest if it is to be effective. For the same reason, this brief time requires a certain intensity in his meeting with God in prayer. It is as though a stranger were to approach me and engage me in conversation, and I were to discover only afterward that it was someone famous. The opportunity would be gone. In much the same way, this time of transition conceals a mystery that will never recur; one who chooses a state of life must be aware of this.

Something similar occurs in the case of one who marries. A young woman was, perhaps, a member of a club or an association of young unmarried women. Now she is engaged and will soon marry. The time for clubs is past. But the remaining members expect something of their former companion, something she is able to give them precisely at this time and that has nothing to do with the nostalgia of farewells. She must find the proper tone for conveying to her companions—and reserving in part for herself—what will be fruitful for both and helpful in shaping the future of both. And she must do this without ambition or vanity, in the humility of prayer. She is indebted to the environment she is leaving for much that has made her choice an easy one. Her gratitude should take a fruitful form that will continue to work, like a seed, in both parties.

It is a special time—even before God. It is a time of responsibility that is distinct in character from the times that precede and follow it. It is truly an epoch in which essentially different times overlap, in much the same way as temporal and eternal time overlap in the sacraments, in the Church's time as such, in the time of Christian life. It is a time in which what is ended and what is just beginning meet in so essential a way that what is past must shed its light on what is to come and what is to come must shed its light on what is past. For those who will marry, the meaning of this time of transition is underscored by society's creation of a special state: the period of their betrothal. But this time exists also and is just as important for those who choose to

dedicate themselves to God and to the service of the
Church. It is not the forty days of the Lord, for he was
preparing himself for public life. It is truly a time that
consists of two times and is therefore all the more fruitful
but also all the more endangered and which must be
lived with all the more discretion.

It is also a time for repairing and retrieving much that
has hitherto been neglected—for example, the relationship with one's parents, with one's brothers and sisters,
with one's friends and comrades. These relationships
should be conducted in such a way that as much as
possible of the future is made living and real ahead of
time. A young woman enters Carmel; her companions
remain behind. Correspondence will be curtailed in the
future and visits will be limited. But those who remain in
the world should know that they will be remembered in
the convent; and the future Carmelite, who knows that
she has been received by God as a handmaiden, will
sincerely desire that something of this spirit live in the
group to which she previously belonged. She lets something of her mystery of union with God shine challeng-
ingly through; whenever the door opens, a light shines
forth. She does not present herself as a model of morality
but only as one who has been chosen by God and who
understands and fulfills God's choice. Everything remains discreet and hidden in prayer, attitude and wish.
Or a young man goes to the missions: he speaks with
genuine gratitude of his debt to the groups and associations to which he belonged. His companions learn
something of the seriousness of Christian election. During this time, people are inclined to be more tolerant
toward the one who is leaving: he can venture to express
himself more openly without being considered indis-

creet. A light shines on him, causing him to stand out from the crowd; everyone understands that it is not he who is important, but God's call and the decision, effected in him by grace, to respond to this call. This subjective element is a delicate issue, but it will endure because it is part of an objective whole, a kind of demonstration of the rightness of the Christian faith.

These things are done properly only if the period of preparation is passed, not in busy haste, but with time left for quiet and recollection. To think seriously about the future requires a special recollection that will not be in the same way necessary or possible at a later date.

In Being

One who makes his choice before God and as the fruit of his contemplation of the divine will, will see clearly that he must adapt himself to this will. Once the call has been heard, once God's will has been recognized and the choice has been made, such a one will usually find himself in a state in which both the will to which he has submitted himself and the submission are genuine but have not yet become coextensive. He has assented to grow into a vocation, and this assent is, of course, the prerequisite for his growth. But all that is present thus far is his declared will to go where God will have him go. This declared will opens the way and even makes part of it visible beforehand. But it is not itself the way. And the submission has yet to be accomplished. It is less the sum of a series of individual actions than the result of a long disposition and a slow growth, the fruit of prayer and of an inner attitude that has adapted itself perfectly to the divine will. It is an attitude by which one veers neither to right nor left to see what other possibilities life has to offer and what else it might include but rather strives always toward the center and seeks only to be exactly in the place that contains the will of God which was assented to fundamentally. What might be called a kind of sampling, especially in prayer—certain daydreams and reflections that are not strictly forbidden and that one generously believes God will shape into something meaningful and fruitful—all this must go, for God has now indicated the fruit he expects. Only the individual's naked submission to the will of God is now acceptable, his pure attempt to become what God wants him to be. If his insight is genuine, it will include in itself the resolution not to stray again from the path but rather to let himself be formed by the path itself, by its un-evenness: so to entrust himself to the hardships, the dangers, the struggles and the incomprehensibility of the path he is called to follow that this path, which is the will of God for him, is his constant law.

As Saint Thérèse of Lisieux so accurately recognizes and describes in teaching her "little way", everything on this path is basically of equal significance. And since everything is of equal importance, everything must be undertaken with equal readiness and equal conformity to the will of God. How widely the pendulum of some-one's emotions swings back and forth is no longer of any significance. Objectively, much can be demanded of him; conformity to a particular point can be especially difficult; it can seem that no ease is in sight and that no progress is being made. On the other hand, he can have the feeling that everything is so filled with grace that he is overwhelmed by it. Actually, however, neither state matters. He must not let his attitude or feelings be influenced by the greatness or smallness of events. What is important is to persevere, to remain firm, to let God's will be done; but I must do so in the awareness that this inner attitude is my answer of obedience to the will of God.

This is especially true of the time after someone has made his choice. What must happen now is what is directly demanded by God, regardless of the ease or difficulty inherent in his vocation itself, in the rule of the religious order or congregation or in the marriage he has chosen to enter. The "old man" must let himself be made into something new even before it has appeared outwardly what this newness is to be; he must reflect his new relationship to God. This relationship is characterized by an immediacy and a defenselessness that he will not know again in this form. Later, the superior, the bishop or his spouse and the routine of family life will take over an important function of this law and provide for his continued vitality. When this happens, his old life will have come to an end, will have passed, by a kind of death, into a new birth. This death, however, should be, not an external ceremony, but something in which he freely cooperates. He must die interiorly if he wants to die exteriorly by his entrance into a particular state of life. Life up to this point has been a training for this dying, a testing of his aptness for it, but a test whose results he will never learn, for it has taken place in the mystery of God.

But he places himself at God's disposal as he now is: still unbound and with a spontaneity that on the one hand flows from the choice he has made and on the other hand is made possible by the fact that he is not yet actually bound to a state of life. That is what makes this time so meritorious. One will also take careful inventory of himself—examining, bringing order, cleaning, as a housewife in springtime takes out and examines even those things that have been laid away and are seldom or never used. One does not know which of them will be needed at a later date, which of them will be useful in marriage or in religious life; hence it is prudent, in the meantime, to attend to all of them. It is a great housecleaning before God. Where something requires attention, he gives it in God's presence, in awareness of his divine will.

In the bridal songs of the Old Testament, in the Song of Songs which depicts the bridal relationship of God through the image of marriage, a single detail that had hitherto seemed insignificant in itself sometimes acquires a sudden meaning by reason of the attention that has been directed to it. God has expectations which the bride does not know in advance, but for which she should be equipped. There are also certain expectations in her which she herself does not completely understand and which God has perhaps placed in her so that he may act as the one who fulfills these expectations. Thus one must accustom oneself to precisely this requirement.

In Further Development

The time of choosing was dominated by man's personal relationship with God, the Church's role being primarily that of dispensing the sacraments and only to a lesser degree that of making direct claims upon the individual. Certainly one encountered the Church everywhere but somehow without any questions being raised. After the choice, however, the Christian enters upon a particular ecclesial form of life, a Christian state of life with its own special rules. During and before his choice it seemed to him that the whole Church belonged to him. She was, of course, God's possession that revealed and communicated him to the world, but she seemed so great that the individual could embrace her only as a whole, without being selective. He could draw from her fullness: receive certain sacraments, practice certain devotions, be more open toward one aspect, more closed toward another, appreciate life within the congregation or to some extent avoid it. But now that he has made his choice and belongs to an ecclesial state of life, all that is changed. The states of life are distinct from one another, and the Church makes her demands upon each one; much that could hitherto have been ignored has now become urgent and demands to be obeyed and put into practice. Obedience was hitherto one of many virtues in the life of faith. To believe in God and to be obedient in general to his commandments seemed to be all the obedience that was required of the Christian. Now, however, obedience reaches more deeply into his personal, private life, into areas that have never before drawn attention to themselves. He must now conform his whole being to what God is demanding of him. And he must do so, not by being increasingly preoccupied with self, but by his response to God which must now become detailed. He must not unduly emphasize these details but must order them into the whole context. Hitherto, perhaps, an individual has given little thought to chastity. Now, however, when he is about to become a priest and wants to preserve his virginity for God, he must give the matter his full attention and know what he is taking upon himself. He cannot dismiss it with a wave of the hand: the question of sex has no interest for me; therefore it is easy for me to preserve my virginity. Another individual has finished secondary school with only a fair degree of success and has perhaps done a bit of studying since then, but without particularly enjoying it. Now he decides to enter an order that will at once require him to devote long years to study. He must change his inner attitude toward studying; it can no longer be something he merely "lives through", that merely "rolls off" him. Or a third individual marries and rejoices in the security of having his own home. But he must also consider the responsibilities he will take upon himself and the sacrifices that family life will require of him. All these insights and adjustments are part of his obedience even now because he is now preparing himself to meet the demands of the state of life chosen for him by God: certainly with the help of grace, but also with what he is himself, his talents and potentials. He cannot count on receiving a grace that will make him responsible almost against his will. He must cooperate with grace if for no other reason than so as not to lose it; he must adapt himself to it and keep pace with it at every point where it seeks to take hold. He must not try to anticipate or correct it but must always be one who seeks only to obey.

Thus the Church appears now in a different light. Formerly she was open; now she closes all her "waiting rooms" to one who has chosen: her clubs for young men, her associations for young women, her study programs, and the like. All of them are closed now, for it is time for the individual to catch the train and, like a traveler, to take the necessary baggage, and no excess. He must take what is suitable for the journey he has in mind: light clothes for the south, heavy shoes for the mountains.

A person's preparedness will also change during the journey. It is not possible to give his assent once for all. The wholeness of his life consists of many parts, and they are what is important now: the parts, and the parts of parts. The world that is revealing itself has theoretical and practical rules of which he was not—could not have been—formerly aware because they had as yet no inner application for him. He looks forward to his wedding day but discovers also the dark side of things: the less attractive qualities of his future spouse and a thousand other obstacles. Enthusiasm for the whole is not enough. The person who has chosen a state of life must live as that state demands. If until now he has had only the whole in view, he must not now narrow his horizons in a petty, trivializing way. But he must realize the whole within his chosen state of life. He will be affected by it precisely in those areas in which he thought he had to remain immutable. As long as he had not yet made his choice, he found joy in painting his future in concrete terms, in a way that appealed to him. But what he has actually chosen will, in any case, be different from this ideal. This would be true even for one who, without choosing a state of life, simply pursued a personal plan: were such a one to look back after twenty years, he would have to admit, if he were honest, that everything had turned out far differently from what he had expected. But the way will be even more dissimilar when it is pursued within a chosen state of life. Hence he must accept from the beginning the fundamental transformation demanded by his state and not try to regulate everything according to a preformed pattern.

If a person of average intelligence undertakes in full freedom to shape his life according to his own plan, he will, of course, realize that he must create a certain order within it, and he will also to some extent subject himself to this order. But that is far from being the obligation assumed by a person who, before God, chooses a state of life within the Church and must endeavor thereafter to shape his life according to this state and to solve in the sight of God whatever questions it raises. Since his choice was made in prayer and prayer offers no easy alternatives, there will no longer be any such in life. At this point he comes to realize that someone who fails to make a choice fails to commit himself, whether he does so by explicit rejection of commitment or by postponing his choice again and again into old age.

IV

Life in One's Chosen State

In One's New Life

A person's new life begins, for the most part, with a belated awareness that the gate has closed behind him. Like the days just before and just after it, the day of his entrance into seminary or novitiate or his wedding day can scarcely be assimilated: it is a swiftly moving series of events that sweeps him along with it and with which he can scarcely keep up. Taken by surprise, exhausted, somehow caught unawares, he is overwhelmed by the fullness of events. He is no longer able to form an opinion about what is happening; he can only let it happen.

The new life begins as something truly new. There is no transition, no gradual adjustment. One who enters the religious life is, of course, informed of the things he must know. But everything is so new and, at the same time, so harmonious that he is simply overpowered by it. Even in the contemplative life with its many hours of meditation, he receives so many guidelines for meditation in the first few weeks that his ability to react is temporarily blunted. Yet he must not relinquish the good resolutions and the adjustments he has already made, or the responsibility and the obligation he has assumed before God with regard to his new state of life.

His surprise must not cause him to lead, from the beginning, a life of routine in which he does what he must do without interior reaction, in which he accomplishes his tasks as quickly as possible and has done with them, in which he adapts himself quickly to the fit of his new clothes and even as a novice—even before he has understood in the least what it is all about—begins to conduct himself like a master.

In the beginning, this is the greatest danger: that precisely because so many new impressions present themselves, the newcomer will assimilate everything only in a general and superficial manner. These impressions belong to his new state of life, but they are to be absorbed interiorly—individually and successively, and not all at once. For his new way of life is not a drill, but the answer of a Christian who has been chosen to the God who has chosen him. There is danger that he will equate and confuse exterior matters—the rules of the house, the daily schedule—with what is interior and essential: that he will so quickly adapt himself to exterior matters that he will overlook those that are interior. He must not try to drink the cream at the very beginning of his new way of life but must be content with what is given him. Many a new seminarian or married man is ill at ease but does not want others to see it; he wants to plunge in at once. But it is not wise to do so.

When the external unrest and pressures of his new and unaccustomed way of life have somewhat abated, the individual begins to realize how much broader his horizon has become by reason of his new life. A new life must always make apparent, in some fashion, the narrowness of the life that one left. The earlier life was narrower because it was not yet a state of life but only a training for it. It is quite possible that an individual will at first find the new rules and regulations, the new horarium and the numerous obligations a burden, an apparent obscuring of what is essential, perhaps even a clipping of the wings of love, which cannot unfold and soar aloft. What is required is so trifling that the great interior gift of self seems somehow too costly to be wasted on it. The individual finds a place in himself for the totality; he has no sense for what is partial. But he must convince himself as quickly as possible that the new life is a more perfect one and that, if he does not yet experience it as such, if he has still many reservations concerning it, the fault lies obviously with himself and not with the state of life. Every individual has not only the right but also the duty to search out what is good in the state he has chosen. If his choice has truly been made in God, then it is also God's will that the individual find fulfillment in the way of life he has chosen. And if that is truly God's perfect will, then this will must be found even in the day-to-day routine of the new life.

The new life can be so strange at first that the individual feels lost. But there is nothing to be gained by constantly looking back, keeping his former self always in tow like an old companion. He must apply his heart and mind to this new way of life in order to discover in it the meaning God intends him to find. Partial demands are to be interpreted in the light of the great, total demand; an assent to God can be divided into any number of parts, yet it always remains a whole.

As the individual gradually becomes aware of the perfection of his state of life, another danger makes its appearance. He begins to regard the way he has chosen as the only valid way. He takes pride in the fact that he has done the right thing, whereas all who have not done as he has are to be pitied. This false superiority, this exclusive emphasis on his own choice, is a sign of immaturity. The individual has succumbed too quickly to the illusion that he understands everything. He has failed to observe that the demand, even when it is satisfied, always reveals the distance between God and man—a revelation, certainly, that occurs in grace, so that the distance does not cast us into despair but rather compels us to that fear of the Lord that is the beginning of wisdom and the foundation of all love. This occurs in the grace that keeps its demand always living before our eyes and spurs us on to ever greater understanding, but interprets this understanding not merely as an act of the intellect but as a matter of one's total attitude, conformity to the divine plan and will. It is an assent that is everywhere expressed in deed and in submission, that divides into individual details and comes together again in God.

A young man wants to become a priest. The daily routine of the seminary requires that he devote his time to certain activities—Gregorian chant, for instance—with which he is already more than familiar. He finds it extremely irritating to have to sing the same passage for the twentieth time. But he is not alone; he belongs now to a seminary community, a diocese. He must play his part in it without showing his companions a disgruntled countenance that would have nothing to do with the present will of God. He must learn to keep a low profile in all the events of life. Perhaps his new life brings him into contact with persons who have not—or have not yet—chosen a state of life. He can certainly encourage them to the choice, but, in doing so, he must never forget that he may not point to himself and his own choice as a model or let his exhortations be tinged by even the slightest suggestion of superiority. What he has chosen is of no benefit to others. And if, before or after his ordination, he is asked to give advice, he must bind men, not to himself, but to God; he must never forget that his poor homilies and admonitions fall infinitely short of what the word of God means in its fullness or of what Christ would have said in his place to those who are now seeking his advice. He must never forget that God sees when his attitude is not pure before God and man; that there is indeed a grace proper to every state of life, but that it has its source in God, not in man. A certain false affability, a certain smugness and unction, a certain extolling of his own way and, incidentally, of himself: all these he must eschew. Nor will he regard doing so as an act of special humility, but as a most ordinary action. Man always wants to revolutionize the world according to his own lights. But the only one who can do this is the Lord, who stands above all the states of life. The Christian has so many obligations that he cannot fulfill in his state of life that this state gives him no right to look down on one whom God's will has perhaps not destined for the same state, but who accomplishes more with a modest allotment of grace than the chosen one has accomplished with all the grace he has received.

The choice was made in prayer between God and the one who sought him. It was possible because the world is as it is at the present time, and because the Church has her special place in it: just so and not otherwise. For this reason, the world and the people in it had their place in the prayer of the one choosing a state of life; they contributed to his vocation both by what they were and

by what they did. To some extent, these people have
familiar faces: he spoke with a friend or with his mother,
and the conversations challenged him and were, to some
extent, responsible for bringing him to his present state.
In addition there are the countless numbers of those
whose faces are not known to him, some of whom will
lose their anonymity by reason of his vocation. As a
priest, he will meet different people than he would have
met if he had remained in the world. Whoever they are,
they will help to shape the course of his life. Thus, people
from the time before and the time after his choice share
in that choice and, to the extent that they contribute
intimately or remotely to its accomplishment, have a
claim on the one who chooses. He is indebted even to
sinners, for they have led him to consider the possibility
of a life lived totally for God, of doing something whole
in one of the ecclesial states of life. When he meets his
fellowmen, then, he has no reason to look down on
them; it is they who have helped to make his way
possible. Perhaps it was the sight of the undisciplined life
of contemporary society that moved him to enter upon a
good marriage. And it was not contempt that inspired
him to that resolution; rather, it was the will to help, to
be a leader for those who often knew no better. He must
not later fall away from his first disposition.

***

His choice was made in prayer; the world's participation
(however discreet) in the choice was possible because the
world had a place in his prayer and was contemplated
there in the presence of God. Now the world must
receive due thanks from his prayer, but the whole life of

the Christian in his new state must also be the expression and confirmation of the choice he has made in prayer. Like his state of life, his attitude toward the people around him must be the outcome of prayer. The prayer proper to his state of life must be the formative element in all things. It must not happen that he chooses his state of life in prayer, but that prayer then has no further role to play in that state. He must not allow himself to feel that by his choice he has somehow reached his destination and established himself. His prayer of choice must be the source of all that follows—not as though the choice itself must be repeated, but in such a way that the prayer made then retains its strength and purity. He must ask of God the grace to persevere in the grace and prayer of his choice. And his perseverance requires no less grace than the choice itself. The choice determined the path he would take; now it is time to follow that path and, in doing so, to leave behind all other paths, but without for that reason rejecting or despising them.

Before his choice he had the option of many ways of life, all of them good, willed by God and formed by the Church. He could choose only one of them, but his choice was made possible by the fact that the other ways were possible of choice—and therefore defensible—and are preferred by other people for good reasons. After his choice, his awareness of the objective goodness and value of the various states of life ought not to change. They are all embraced by the one Church, which has need of them and protects them in their diversity; they, in their turn, have need of the Church and her prayer; and everyone who has made his choice is part of the Church and must contribute to the totality of her prayer. This glance at the whole, at the Church in her totality, is the best protection against smugness and helps to keep alive the original grace of one's state. This does not mean that prayer now offers the same consolation as it did in the beginning, at the time of choice. Then, perhaps, the consolation was part of God's purpose, designed to give the one choosing certainty and to confirm him in his choice. Later, God withdraws his consolation so that the Christian is drawn imperceptibly into the state of sacrifice. This change in prayer is integral to his state of life; it is a sign from God that matters are serious now, that his service of God has begun and both reflection and gratification are withdrawn. A corresponding change in the Christian's readiness to serve is also to be expected because God is constantly claiming and awakening different aspects of his readiness. It is his duty, now, to be adaptable both in his response to the demands of this service and in the form that his readiness to serve will take at any given time.

***

One who has made his choice differs from one who has not in that his choice now lies behind him. But for this "behind" there is always a corresponding "before", a becoming. Properly speaking, the further he is from the moment of choice, the more fully he must dedicate himself to his chosen way of life. It is part of the choice's character as prayer that it is to take effect in the chosen life in an ever greater and ever more refreshing way. With every step he takes, the horizon broadens; new images appear, altering the circumstances of his life. Even if he experiences a long period of dryness in prayer, he must continue to strive with all his might to change whatever needs correction in his relationship with his neighbor and his environment. The pendulum of faith must continue to swing freely even though his life has, to all appearances, come to rest.

In addition, the process of choosing is often accompanied by a certain curiosity and expectation. One wants to ask God many questions—questions about one's own fitness or about God's wish to put one in precisely this place or to make precisely that demand of one. One must not grow weary of this questioning. To one's thousands of questions, God answers with a single, all-embracing Yes, and this Yes was already spoken before the questions were asked, for God chose me from all eternity in the expectation that I would ask these questions. And, without noticing it, I am drawn by my questions into his eternally prepared Yes. At the time of choosing, I asked the questions proper to the state in which I found myself; I expected that God would, at each moment, give the answer most suited to my question. I asked: Will you be able to use me? And God said: Yes, with the help of my grace. I asked: Will I be of use to you? And again God said: Yes, with the help of my grace. I thought my questions were somewhat differentiated, but they were all answered by God's ever-present Yes. His Yes was the answer to everything. But that same Yes was also, even then, an answer in advance to the questions I would ask later in life. And if I try to form other questions, to represent the difficulties I experience, to deepen my awareness of God's demands upon me, he still answers with that same Yes. This does not free me from the obligation of perpetually meeting God's Yes anew and as though for the first time—nor, therefore, of the obligation of phrasing my questions in such a way that I am

justified in addressing them to this Yes. My questions
are the expression of my being in its present circumstances. But this being, which has been placed in God's
service, is transformed by God in whatever way his
answer requires. Hence my relationship to God is not
without reference to the transformation he constantly
works upon me in order that I may always experience his
open Yes of grace as the correct object of my questions.

One's state of life bears the mark imprinted upon it by
the Lord and by the Church, a mark that is always living
because the Lord and the Church are the source of life.
But one's state of life gives rise to innumerable questions
even while it provides answers to innumerable others,
answers that spring from the dialogue between the Lord
and his Bride. In every ecclesial state of life there is a kind
of foundation on which rests the relationship of the
particular state to the general state that is the Church—
a relationship which is therefore comparable in many
ways to that between Bride and Bridegroom, between
Christ and the Church, where the Church is represented
by the particular state of life and the Lord by the Church.
This dialogue between Bride and Bridegroom is not cold
or stiff; it draws its life from the word of God that is
bestowed upon it, that is, from the God-Word himself,
the Son. This word is perceptible wherever the state of
life is, and it is at the service of those who live in that
state. It is like the Bridegroom's wedding gift to the
Bride, the true consequence of the Lord's choice, who
has himself chosen the Church as his Bride and in her has
ensured to all the faithful a participation in his own
nature. If the Son did not have the Church, no dialogue
would be possible. But because he is always with the
Church, the dialogue is audible wherever the Church is

present in her states of life, preserving the word of God for and bestowing it upon those who have made their choice. The dialogue within a given state of life contains mysteries that are accessible only to those who are in that state. Those outside it can never begin to imagine the reality of what takes place between God and the one he has called. They can, of course, have some inkling of it and be aware of some part of it; but even when the requirement has been met that everyone live in the state destined for him by God, when all Christians unite to form, in the midst of mankind, a community of saints that is the Church, there still remains a sphere that is proper to each state and is its particular secret with God. In spite of and even because of this secret, however, the religious will have for the married man, as the married man will for the priest, an inner understanding and closeness that one who has never chosen cannot possibly have for other people. One who has made his choice put himself by that choice at the place where God waits to speak with him, where the word of God's love is perceptible to him and where he, understanding this word as God means him to understand it and obeying the will of God for him, can proclaim it to others according to God's will, in a way similar to the way in which the Son fulfilled the will of the Father by proclaiming the Father's word to the Apostles and making it take effect in them.

In the Chosen State

If it is permissible to speak analogously of a *"state"* in *God* and to regard the communality of the three Divine Persons in the one nature of God as their "state", then it is possible to ascribe to the Word, the Son who is begotten of the Father from all eternity, a fundamental role in this "state": for he is the expression of the divine conversation. He is at once Son and Word. Since he is eternally in the situation of standing before the Father, as he is one with the will of the Father and with the love of the Holy Spirit and places himself with them at the service of the world, it would be difficult to distinguish between the word he utters and the Word he is. He manifests this unity by his ever new procession from the Father, by his silence and by his utterances, by his eternal issuing from and returning to the Father. And because he is generated by the Father and because the Holy Spirit proceeds from both of them, he forms a kind of center of exchange: he unites the trinitarian life because he is the Word that both expresses the Father and embraces and returns to him in the love of the Spirit. Both the one nature and the trinity of Persons are eternal. Through the one nature courses the love that also courses through the divine "state"; for God's "state" [*Stand*] is not something fixed and rigid, but rather that eternal "permanency" [*Bestand*] that forms and contains the eternal life of God.

A child is the expression and evidence of the fruitfulness of husband and wife. One seeks to find in the child resemblance to the parents. For the world, the child is the seal and the summary of the parents' married state. For the parents themselves, on the other hand, he is the expression of their love, a personal love between husband and wife that is now enriched by the personal love of each parent for the child. The child, in turn, loves both parents as a unit, although he may turn in conversation now to the father, now to the mother, both of whom he loves as individual persons.

God the Father is for the Son what father and mother are for the human child: the source of both his nature and his personal being. The Son loves the Father as his procreator, who is at once the Person of the Father and God—absolute God, who has no need to emphasize his paternal character in order to show that he is God. And since the Father and Son breathe forth the Holy Spirit from all eternity, the Son loves both the Father and the Spirit. The Spirit loves the Father and the Son with a love analogous to that with which we love father and mother: both in their oneness as the principle that generates and sends forth, and in their individuality as Persons. But the occasion of this differentiation is the Son, who, in his procession from the Father, makes the divine "state" visible. To say that the Father generates the Son from all eternity and that the Spirit proceeds from all eternity from the Father and the Son is to reveal the dynamism of the divine state. It is an eternal existence that lacks nothing and whose fullness is expressed in this eternal generation and eternal life.

It is clear from all this that a Christian state of life must have an inner dynamism if it is to be in the image of God. The traditional states within the Church have always constituted a dynamic way of life to which the individual must give his consent. Only from this perspective can we understand how a person can assent to a state of life and persevere in it for a lifetime. Even from the perspective of faith, it would be impossible for him to do so if his acceptance of his state were not flexible and adaptable, if his being were not open to becoming. To assent to a state of life that was only a state of rest would be tantamount to burying himself alive. But in God life is embedded in eternal being, and in us being is dependent on becoming. If we are to remain alive in our state of life, that state must receive and retain its dynamism from God. The vitality comes from God; it is conferred on the state, which must accept it. Hence God's eternal state of being moved is translated into dynamism within the state of life. But it does not stop at this translation. In the grace proper to a given state, it continues also to bestow a share in eternal life.

By himself, man would be incapable of meeting God's vitality directly, unshielded and, as it were, unprotected. He would inevitably be consumed by this fire and would have to surrender his spirit. The naked fire of God must be joined by a principle of order. This is the raison d'être of the Church and, within the Church, of the states of life. They guard God's life within themselves. Within this order there is a certain division of roles, and one must make one's choice among them. For the Christian, however, decision is never an evasion: therefore it is not permitted one who has made his choice to try later to escape the divine fire. They would do well to consider this fact who, from the three states of life, choose only the form of a particular state without regard to its content.

***

When God created the world and entrusted it to *Adam*, the bestowal was the expression of a twofold divine love: God's love for man, whom he had just created, and the intradivine love. We can say that the Father created the world out of love for his Son, and perhaps even—for this, too, can be substantiated—that he brought it forth knowing that the Son would give it back to him through his Passion. What concerns us here, however, is the love of God the Father for Adam, a love bestowed simultaneously on the Son and on Adam, on the Holy Spirit and on Adam. It is thus a twofold love, which, though it never loses its oneness, must return to it again and again because it is directed to a twofold object, to both God and the creature—a love that is dynamic even when it is directed to Adam alone because it issues from the eternal activity of the Trinity. The intradivine "state" is an expression of love. The fact that in God the three Divine Persons are distinct and separate from one another is an expression of love. And there is something present in the movement of love from one Person to the other that belongs to the divine "state" from all eternity and in which the existence of this "state" is perceived. We might express it thus: having God himself as its vessel, divine love assumes the form of this vessel; in its perduring and in all its expressions and forms it points always to this vessel, the divine nature. Every word calls attention to the work, every moment to eternity, every grace to God. In founding the Church, it was the Son's intention to infuse into her something of this "state". He distributed divine love among the ecclesial states in such a way that the states received it as their formative principle and, in the very act of receiving it, became what they are: states of life. God bestows his love on the Church through the various states of life as through a variety of vessels, each of which reflects something of the original divine vessel and contains love in its entirety, but always in the way intended for and proper to the particular state.

In paradise, there was only *one* state of life. At the disposal of this one state, which was the human state, God placed all the divine love he had ordained for what would eventually be the individual states of life, bestowing it, not according to rules, but only according to need.

This total openness on God's part had as its prerequisite man's perfect openness to God. Man was indeed placed in time, in a predictable sequence of day and night; time was given him that he might become oriented and comfortable in existence. He was not immediately confronted with all eternity. Even the things of this world were presented to him and his human understanding in a way he could comprehend. He would have emerged eventually from this earthly day into eternal day and from this earthly life into eternal life. All that was earthly would have been an introduction to, an anticipatory experiencing of—as it were, a novitiate for—eternity. Man's time in paradise would have been a time of preparation for eternal life, which is God the Creator's own time. His life on earth would have been a time of assimilation, made easy for him, to this incredible and eternal initiative of the Creator.[1]

With the founding of the *Church* in the New Testament, God makes even more of his divine life visible to mankind. He reveals some of the differentiation in the divine state in order to form the states in the Church. The Church is instituted as mediatrix between the divine life and sin-laden, God-alienated human life in order to ease man's approach to God. Without the Church, man would not only have no proper understanding of the Father when he speaks from heaven as he did in the Old Testament; he would also fail to understand the Son

[1] For a more detailed discussion of the derivation of the individual states of life within the Church from man's post-paradisal existence, cf. Adrienne von Speyr's still unpublished works on the theology of the sexes, on marriage and virginity, and on Christology and the Church.—Ed.

when he speaks to men on earth about the things of heaven. An organism that is at the same time the Bride of the Son is required if the words, actions, mysteries and graces of the Son are to be objectively safeguarded and mediated. In this respect, the role of the Church is very close to that of the Mother of the Lord. Men would not understand the Son if he did not have an earthly mother. And they would have failed to understand him after his death if he had not established the Church as his earthly steward.

The sacraments are the ecclesial modes of access to divine life. On the one hand, they enhance and elevate the forms and destinies of human life by the grace they bestow; on the other hand, they are the forms by which divine grace enters into man's life. The ecclesial states are a further development of these modes of access. They, too, elevate man's natural dispositions and forms of life and also place themselves between the dispensation and the reception of the sacraments as a medium that both confirms and adapts.

***

After the creation of Eve, God's twofold love—his love as it exists within the Trinity and his love for mankind whom he had created—was reflected in Adam in a two-fold love for God and for the woman. Because he had been created in solitude, Adam was not naturally disposed to love his fellowman; his love was directed primarily to God. And it somehow seems that the sudden creation of Eve shook him so that he could not distinguish between his love for her and his love for God, and was thus more easily tempted by Eve. But this love for his fellowman was always potentially present in Adam, and it became a reality through Eve. Adam learns to love Eve on the model of the divine love: as the other person who shared his human nature, just as God's love has its source at once in his Person and in his nature. Even the mysteries of fruitfulness that begin between husband and wife are images of the trinitarian mystery within the Godhead.

This is the origin of the *first differentiation* of the ecclesial states of life. The married state emphasizes the love between two human persons. The state of virginity (which now includes the evangelical and priestly states) emphasizes above all man's love for God. Through his love for another person, man finds in marriage new access to God; through his love for God, the celibate person finds a new access to mankind. In one sense, then, married love more strongly indicates divine love as it is revealed in the Persons of the Trinity, whereas virginal love more strongly indicates that same love as it is revealed in the nature of God. Hence the love of God reveals itself more fully within the framework of the Church than in the Old Testament. This is not to say, however, that the state of virginity offers a vaguer knowledge of the love of the three Divine Persons in God than does the married state: because of the choice, the opposite must be true. Because the virgin chooses God as the true Thou of his life, the divine nature is revealed to him in personal fashion. The married man, on the contrary, finds his Thou primarily in a fellow human being; he does not know God so much directly as through his spouse. God's Personhood manifests itself to him through another human person. This shows a way in which the state of virginity is superior.

In this first relation we cannot yet speak of the priest-hood as a separate, third possibility. It was not Adam, but Abel—an Abel already subject to the law of original sin, sacrifice and reconciliation—who was a "priest" as the term is understood in salvation history. The priestly state is related to God's state (the evangelical state) and to the human (married) state as the ecclesial office is related to the Christian mission and to Christian love: as a crystallization, coming about only after the establishment of original sin, of one aspect of man's fluid life.

***

One who approaches the choice of a Christian state of life for the first time has not yet experienced any important pattern and continuity of life. He chooses something and has some instructions for its use; but it is only by actual use that he will be able to test and know the meaning and utility of the instructions. Choose he must: he bows to this necessity and makes his choice but remains, at least for the time being, the same person he was, molded by life in precisely this way and provided with precisely these qualities. And it is precisely as this person that he turns to the new way of life that is a necessity for him, though not yet a genuine experience. Only with his first experience of it, during which the value of the new way of life is confirmed, only with the accompanying dialogue with God does there arise in him a personal awareness of his new position, of the position of his new state of life. This state now begins to reveal its inner logic, its vitality, its intimate union with God, its radiance in the Church and in the person's own life. The human person is changed by belonging to a state of life;

his relationship to the Church and to God is colored and transformed by his newly awakened consciousness of and responsibility toward his state, and by his awareness of the bond that links him to those who share it. Only now, when he no longer views the fruit from a distance but has actually bitten into it, does he know its taste. It is not enough to embrace one's vocation and state of life; one must also be embraced by them. Only then do they reveal their inner reality, their significance, their beauty. Certainly the decision to enter a particular state had its source in a certain affinity for that way of life. But this way was not yet to be found in him who chose it; it was hidden in God and in his voice. Now the individual has become the representative, indeed the object, of his state of life: not as though something strange had happened to him, but rather in such a way that he feels responsible before God for this objective, all-encompassing experience. His journey has begun; the surrounding countryside has changed. But he was prepared for that and must now accept the consequences of his decision, like an explorer who has made all kinds of preparations for his expedition. All is changed, however, when he finds himself at last in the region to be explored. For he is no longer master of the situation as he was when he was sitting at his desk, but finds himself affected and influenced by the things around him. Some of his preparations prove now to have been mere ballast; others were either overlooked or could not have been foreseen. He is astonished now that he did not think of them. The reports of earlier travelers prove to have been incomplete in many respects. Perhaps they were not even aware of the things that are the chief sources of difficulty on this trip. . . .

Even after one has entered upon a chosen state of life, one has still the obligation of realizing—of experiencing the reality of—the life of faith and the content of that faith. Before his choice, the individual can be pious and filled with faith; he stands in the midst of a fallen world that longs for redemption, and the longer he lives, the more aware he becomes that it is in need of redemption. As a Christian he knows that the Son reconciled the world to God by his death on the Cross. But the perspective from which he views both God and the world is predominantly one of observation and contemplation. He registers, as it were, what God does and what the world does, and he is thus able, to some extent, to measure their respective strength: the *modus operandi* of grace and, to a lesser degree, that of sin, and that of the Christian as well, but always from the perspective of an outside observer. After his choice, he is in the midst of the fray—in the very process of redemption. He is an agent who is also acted upon. And the process is divided in a practical way: various forms of participation are defined by and contained within the different states of life. These are the concrete ways not only of believing in the Lord but also of being on his side and fighting for him. In being thus transformed by his state of life, the Christian learns things that belong so entirely to the intimate world of the Son that they are actually comprehensible only in a trinitarian context.

Until the choice has been made, there is only a gradual approach. The individual avoids committing himself totally or expending too much of his powers. For that reason, his vision of things remains rigid and linear. Acceptance and rejection both refer to this vision. He stands apart from the various parties like a referee in a sports stadium. Even if his sympathies are actually with one side or the other, he owes it to himself to view the proceedings impartially. Nevertheless, the young person cannot help feeling somewhat laughable when he attempts to speak with the full weight of his personality. For he has as yet reached no decision. His "thus" could just as well be something else. As yet he has accomplished nothing. The fact that he later finds himself "all the way in" is a sign that he has meanwhile come to a decision. His vision is no longer flat but stereoscopic and plastic. His state of life opens to him the dimension of depth. Now he no longer watches while others eat; he eats with them. He takes what nourishment he needs for the struggle of his state of life. This is the way to come to a better understanding of God even in the revelation of his depths, to learn more about his triune exchange of life and about his creative actions and purposes. The Christian's cooperation with the Lord is absorbed more deeply into the Son's unity of operation with the Father and the Holy Spirit.

The Christian who has not yet made his decision can turn devoutly in prayer to all three Persons of the Blessed Trinity, honor the saints and fulfill his Christian duties. But his religious exercises are always somehow tangential; they do not yet share fully in this final relationship of God to God. When the Lord called his Apostles and let them cooperate in his ministry, he drew them into his mysteries. They received much more: they understood more about his nature, his Godhead, his union with the Father, his guidance by the Holy Spirit and his aspirations as God and man than do those who merely listen to a sermon and apply some part of it to their own lives, who undergo a form of conversion without advancing to the full following of Christ. On the other hand, the choice of a state of life, properly made, is always a response to the Lord's call so that those called find themselves afterward in a much closer relationship to the Lord. He lives in them by virtue of their choice, which has been made through him and with him. One who is not prepared to make a Christian choice because he regards freedom as his highest good nevertheless creates for himself, in the context of his refusal, certain obligations and responsibilities—but they are not those ordained for him by the Lord. Even the faithful who cannot decide on or are constantly postponing their choice of a state of life until it is too late often create for themselves artificial tasks or obstacles and pretended responsibilities that have nothing to do with the real will of God for them and are not unlike the tasks the non-believer creates for himself within the context of his sin. In the end, these tasks reveal their emptiness because they lack the divine sustenance proper to a legitimate state of life. One who chooses in a Christian manner finds new burdens laid upon him by the Lord. That he may know that they are truly from God, God lets him see more of the mystery of the triune life. God himself assumes responsibility for enabling the Christian to carry out his mission in maturity and full growth of the spirit.

A young man of fifteen may be enthusiastic about everything good and may have the will to serve God. He can even feed for many years from his youthful enthusiasm, sating himself with what God and the world have to offer. Eventually he must make his choice. If he avoids doing so, he may be able, for a time, to sustain his early enthusiasm by artificial means. But in the end he will realize that he cannot live on this enthusiasm alone. For it is a sustenance provided no longer by God, but rather by his own ego, which feeds upon itself. And God is not to be found in this circulation.

***

It is possible to examine in turn each of the individual states of life to discover how each of them brings the Christian who belongs to it closer to the mystery of the triune life. God's nature cannot be defined; we gain the most living access to it through the revelation of the Son, who has made the triune life known to us. Inasmuch as the Father, Son and Holy Spirit are distinct from one another and have each his own particular function within the Godhead, there exists, in the endless ocean of the divine being and the divine properties—that, for us, all seem to converge and coalesce and to be equally removed from us—an order, a plan, and hence a relationship to us. If we had only that ocean of endless properties before our eyes, we would indeed have to say: This immensity, this incomprehensibility, is God. But it would not be the God of creation, not the God of the Cross or of our redemption, not the God of mission; we would find in such a god none of the special characteristics by which he has made himself known to man. He would be a god unapproachable in his oneness.

But because God in his nature is triune and excludes for himself the possibility of being singular and inaccessible, and because he reveals himself to us in a triune mystery, we understand that it belongs to his nature to know *consideration*. God is considerate of God. God loves

God in the loving responsibility of God. There is in him both an embracing and a being embraced that are intrinsic to his nature and that he shows to us. Indeed, he shares this property of his divine "state of life" with the three ecclesial states.

If rightly chosen, the *married state* can be lived to perfection in a family life that is in complete accord with Christian faith and with a position in Church, community and state that is in complete accord with the mind of the Church. In the partnership of husband and wife, in the subjection of both to the law of the family and of the family to the larger units of society, such a state would be an image of trinitarian consideration and inclusion as they are revealed in Christ's gospel. This subjection is both a general one, rendered once and for all within the framework of one's life, and a particular one that daily and hourly requires new acts of consideration. Nevertheless, there are certain limits here that cannot be moved and that simply are related to the finiteness of the human person. Although the grace of marriage extends these limits and establishes them more deeply in God, they continue to exist and often make their presence known, above all in one's fellowman, who in this way provides one with an image and mirror of one's own limitedness. This is not to say that a genuinely Christian marriage does not show signs everywhere of the imitation of the triune love and that something like a further permission for participation in this love cannot be revealed in such a marriage. Nonetheless, certain of God's revelations, and especially those that are related to the office in general and the mystery of Mary's office, actually reveal themselves only in the state of the evangelical counsels.

The *evangelical state*, whether active or contemplative,

gives evidence from the beginning of a stronger pre-occupation with God. God is, in every respect, the goal of this state of life: the individual chooses that form of life that frees him for God. By the study of theology, whether for a long or short time, his understanding and his whole soul with all its longing and striving are directed to God. The image of God grows continually richer, at once more and less comprehensible; the triune dynamism of the divine nature makes a deeper and deeper impression. In marriage, the individual must forego these helps proper to the evangelical state. If it were possible to compare at the end of their lives two individuals who, at the moment of choice, possessed exactly the same qualifications, the same education and knowledge, the same piety and readiness to follow Christ, and of whom one chose the married state and the other the evangelical state, the advantage enjoyed by the latter would be plainly visible. The lay person, including the married person, is engaged in a constant struggle for perseverance before God; the things of this world are always threatening to usurp his attention and to claim it so completely for themselves that he will lose all contact with God. He is more deeply embedded in the consequences of original sin. One in the evangelical state, on the other hand, lives closer to God by reason of the counsels and his own spiritual preoccupation with the things of God. It is easier for him, in his striving and struggling, to keep God's image before his eyes as something living. His state of life is more supernatural; that is, it incorporates many elements of the divine triune life that can be transformed into a dynamic Christian life if he cooperates with grace. It is a life lived at the point where the Son extends his invitation to a special and exclusive discipleship, a life of perfect fulfillment of the Father's will under the guidance and inspiration of the Holy Spirit. Although there is a level on which the ecclesial states stand side by side as possible modes of a Christian existence that are both good and willed by God, there is also a hierarchy among the states that clearly reveals the greater excellence of the evangelical state.

Nor can one overlook the fact that most decisions to enter the married state are less clearly and unambiguously Christian in character than is a decision to enter the evangelical or priestly state. One who chooses either of the latter states is compelled from the beginning to cast himself into the arms of grace and to entrust his cause to grace. One who chooses the married state, on the other hand, must rely and build more strongly on his own strength and reserves. The way in which those in the evangelical state count on grace is not presumption or lack of understanding or excess of confidence, but something rooted deeply in the act of faith. The evangelical state lives from Mary's Yes to the angel and, through the angel, to God; the married state has its Christian beginnings in Joseph's obedience to the divine instruction not to divorce Mary. Both are acts of obedience, but the superiority of the first emerges clearly.

The same is true if we regard the states of life from the perspective of the Son: he himself lives the life of the counsels and invites those who "want to be perfect" to follow him. He shows how perfectly a man—and he is himself this man—can live the divine counsels in this world, and he shows it above all from the perspective of obedience. It is entirely a question of "not my will but thine be done." The Father precedes the Son; he is the "superior" of the Son, whom he sends and who fulfills his mission on earth through the Holy Spirit. By the death that is an integral part of his mission and is led up to by a life lived according to the evangelical counsels, the Son returns to the Father as one coming to give an account of what he has done. Poverty and chastity are included, as if in one vow, in the obedience the Son promises the Father at the Incarnation. When the Son makes the evangelical life accessible to his disciples, he also renders an account, as it were, of the bond that links him as man to the Father in the Holy Spirit. His perfect bond with the Father is at once an external revelation of the life of the Trinity and the founding of the evangelical state in the Church. He gives his followers an example of what perfection is on earth, and he does this super-abundantly by binding himself to God with his whole Person and freedom, thus becoming himself the archetype of the evangelical state.

The married state originates in the Old Covenant, under which man normally was married. Only as an exception, conditional and limited, was a renunciation decreed or imposed by God. By making it a sacrament, the Son elevates the married state, assumed from the Old Covenant, to an ecclesial state of life. He does so in respectful acknowledgment of the Father's work of creation by including the natural and Old Testament form of life in his order of redemption. Married people should not feel like disadvantaged persons or outcasts. Particularly if they chose their path as the right one in prayer, they should receive through the Son a share in what is the Father's, just as, in the Old Covenant, they already had a share through the Father in what is the Son's (because every promise flows into his fulfillment). But they will not receive a share in what is the Spirit's in the same way that the religious does, because the choice of exclusive imitation of the Son results in a particular way from the inspiration of the Spirit who proceeds from both the Father and the Son, and because the evangelical state gives a share in the Son's directness to the Father, which is in a particular way the exchange of the Spirit between the two.

The Apostles had their roots in the Old Testament, and most of them were married. Nevertheless, they "left all things" to follow the Lord. They represent, as it were, a middle position between the married state and the state of the counsels—a position that owes its origin, on the one hand, to their particular historical situation and, on the other, to the fact that their call to follow Christ was chiefly for the sake of taking on the office. It was the Lord's will to found the Church, and on the occasion of this founding Peter and the other Apostles received their ministry. But ministry is always an instrument of mediation and of transmission. The *priesthood* has retained something of this quality throughout the ages. In the Old Testament, married persons looked first to the Father as the creator and progenitor of the Son; in the New Testament, religious look first to the Son, adopting his way of life as their subjective life form. Priests look first to the Church established by the Son and receive through her a share in the triune life. The light of the Holy Spirit that the Apostles and their successors receive for the performance of their ministry is, as it were, a reflected light: it is not the direct radiance of the Trinity but a light shed upon the Church, a light that belongs to the house of God on earth. It is the Holy Spirit of that which *is*; and it is through that which is that priests come to experience, in the same Holy Spirit, that which is *becoming*. Through both, they are introduced into the life of the Trinity. They are defenders of an objective idea rather than of a subjective way or state. Their office, too, is predominantly an expression of the ideal. They affirm that the Virgin has conceived, but they themselves stand neither in the place of Christ nor in that of John. They perceive and identify the holiness that is always a revelation of the triune life of God in order that they may guide, protect and develop it in the service of God.

Every ecclesial state of life lives God's commandment to love one's neighbor in the love of God, which is the reflection on earth of the consideration of God for God within the Trinity. The married man is not alone; he must constantly be aware of his spouse, his children, the family as a whole, his relatives, his place of work, his country. He cannot think and plan as an individual; he is bound to the human community with every fiber of his being. So, too, is one in the evangelical state, but in a different way. He has the order or congregation to which he belongs and through which the Church as a whole receives a special concreteness for him. He is opened by his state of life and his rule to the communal life of the triune God. With the Son, he must at every moment accomplish the will of the Father that is made known to him by the suggestions and inspirations of the Holy Spirit. Thus an infinitely rich field of considerate love opens and expands from God to Christ, to the Church as a whole, to the religious order or congregation and

finally to the individual. It reaches into the depths of the
heavenly mysteries and has, from there, a prominent
share in the mysteries of the real and efficacious possession of heaven on earth, of redemption for a world in
need of redemption. The priesthood stands between the
other two states of life in a middle position that is
not one of synthesis, not a "golden mean", but rather
that mediation which is the specific function of the
office. It becomes apparent at this point that the office, if
considered abstractly and purely in itself, is not sufficient
to develop a separate form of life. Thus the priesthood,
in its concrete form, must always depend on one or both
of the remaining two states, without becoming fully a
part of either. As a result, the priestly life often involves a
loneliness and a certain abstractness that the priest must
combat by an increased outpouring of considerate love.
If he fails to do so, there is danger that his state may
degenerate into the legalism of the Old Testament and
that his celibacy may degenerate into old-maidishness. If
his life is to be commensurate with the content of the
mysteries it is his duty to administer, he must seek to
realize as much as possible within the framework of his
state the spiritual openness to the life of the Trinity that is
characteristic of the evangelical life.

* * *

The mediation of divine life to the ecclesial states of life
by the incarnate Son identifies him as the *Word*. The
states of life are summed up in the Word that is Christ.

The Son, who is begotten of the Father as the Second
Person of the Trinity, faces the Father, founding that
separation [*Ab-stand*] in God that finds its completion

in the separation of the Holy Spirit and that, precisely through this state of separateness, allows the inner breadth of the divine nature to be made manifest to God himself. The trinitarian unity of nature is the most impenetrable of all mysteries, yet nothing becomes light except in its light. As the begetter, the Father is the totality of the infinite Godhead that communicates itself. When the Son stands before the Father (from all eternity) as he who is begotten, the Person of the Father is everything in God that the Person of the Son is not. The same is true of the procession of the Holy Spirit. Precisely in the nonidentity of the Persons is revealed the identity of the divine nature and "state".

And now, in our human community, the Son exemplifies for us, insofar as this is possible, the life of the divine community. He does two things at once: he causes the distinction of Persons to be made known and their function to become visible, and in doing so he affords a deeper insight into their communal existence. Together, these revelations make him, for us, the Word of the Father and the Word of God, the expression of God par excellence. The separateness that exists within the Godhead becomes manifest to us through the separateness of the Incarnation—through the Word's becoming flesh—to the extent to which the Son, as man, is not separated from the Father and does not in any way experience that alienation that sinful creatures have introduced by their turning away from the divine origin. The distance between God and man that is inherent in man's nature is bridged by the Son when, as man, he lives and rests perfectly in the will of the Father, takes his place once and for all in this will and thus makes the distance that separates the creature from God a revelation of the separateness of eternal love and eternal life within the Godhead. Thus we receive a totally new perception of the Father as Person even as we gain insight into the divine state. So long as we preserve this insight, the Son will be for us the Word: the Word as Person, who makes known to us the Persons in God, and the Word as God, who expresses for us the nature of God. The picture he gives us of God is not darkened by sin, yet it is comprehensible to us men through the grace that emanates from him and takes possession of us. Every word spoken by the Son on earth, even when he is speaking to the Father, is something meaningful and perceptible to us; every word reshapes the image of God afresh around a new and revealing center.

But it is not the Son's intention to keep his being the Word of God selfishly to himself. In founding the Church and designing her from the beginning as a differentiated supernatural community, he bestows on her something of this function as Word. He calls the Apostles. He is his Mother's Son and assigns her a special place in his work of redemption. He converts the sinner, Magdalen, and gives her a particular function in the Church and in relation to the Apostles. He calls Paul, the Apostle to the Gentiles. He makes John the beloved disciple. He creates within the Church positions that are distinct from one another and that reveal, by their interrelationships, the absolute unity of the Catholic Church. And he does this not merely through the missions and tasks he assigns to individuals but also through the states of life, which point to the ecclesial state as a whole and, consequently, to Christ, who is the source and goal of the states of life, and ultimately to God. Thus someone who lives in an ecclesial state by reason of a free decision made in faith and prayer stands in a new relationship to the Son as Word. His life in the state will be stamped with the mark of the Word. And the more freshly he hears the word of the Son each day, the more meaningful will his life in the chosen state appear to him each day. There is not only an assimilation of the individual person to the divine Word but also, supporting and including this effort, the further assimilation required by the Son— the constantly renewed assimilation of the state to himself. Just as the demands God makes of a child are different from those he makes of a mature man or of an elderly person, and just as all God's demands to children, however personal they may be, still have certain common elements, so it is with the demands of one's state of life. But man is not immured in his state of life. The child matures gradually into a man; the man becomes old. The states of life do not flow into one another, but life in a given state is never a matter of having arrived; on the contrary, it is a daily seeking and finding. The Son lives in the will of the Father, but he lives for the hour which is not yet come, the knowledge and control of which he leaves to the Father alone. He combines perfection in every moment with an expectation, a striving toward the future. His word takes this form. And our living of a particular state of life must also take this form: a standing firm in the life we have chosen with no slackening of the effort needed to do so. Once we have discovered this secret in the Son, we become aware of the extent to which his word is the "Ever-Greater", enveloped in a breath of triune mystery, that must be reflected in our life of discipleship by an ever new and open readiness before God. Both the assimilation of the individual and that of the state of life to the will of God often make their own demands that nonetheless always have considerable relevance for one's following of the Son as Word—a following that receives here its first full witness. The assimilation penetrates the very center of our being, but this center, which is that of our person as well as of our state of life, somehow has its place in the center of the Church, which, in turn, has her center in the Lord. And this encounter and intersecting of planes is the sign of a grace-filled vitality.

The word of the Son is always both a demand on us and an expression of the way things are. By uniting them in itself, the word overcomes the tension between what should be and what is. It addresses itself to us and places us where we ought to be; it addresses itself to the Father and is fully understood by him. We understand it only imperfectly. Between God's full and our partial understanding lies our life as Christians. But the Word, who is eternally with the Father in his divine fullness and who, in the Incarnation, fulfills the will of the Father by his human striving on earth, bridges the tension by his personal and unique union of God and man. Thus Jesus Christ becomes the principle of all human striving, for he is the striving that is not only fulfilled but also recognized and accepted by God: a striving that seeks fulfillment on earth and finds it in heaven. Christ's striving on earth is a genuinely human striving that possesses nonetheless, and even in the Passion and abandonment, a certainty and imperturbability that have their source in eternity. He fulfills the will of the Father and in doing so *experiences* fulfillment. He brings it about and it becomes his portion. It is here that we sinners and failures have our place. For it is here that the Word, who is the Son, is entrusted to us; here the Lord makes us

sharers in the divine dialogue; here we, too, are permitted to join our lives to the strength of his nature as
Word. In receiving from him the strength to live as
persons, we receive also the strength to heed the word of
God; we are enabled by the word itself to emerge from
our own fumbling, our own uncertainty, into the certainty of the Word of God. The Son does not doubt the
Father. He always sees his path that leads him back to
the Father. His divine infallibility is always incorporated
into his divine-human obedience. Without the strength
and infallibility of the Word who became man for us, we
would be unable to obey God. The Word makes us
obedient. The Word shows us the divine will. The Word
gives us the infallibility of faith, of the Christian way, of
the way of mission, whatever form it may take. In his
ecclesial state, each individual discovers and receives in
the Word the summation of his state and the assurance of
his own perseverance in it. But there is no single word of
God that we can comprehend once and for all. The word
is there that we may return to it and find our support in
it. It gives us assurance, but no guarantee; and the
assurance it gives must constantly be renewed and grow.
If we were to regard any word of God as no longer
significant for us, it would be a sign that our spirit had
begun to die. For, as long as he breathes within us, the
Holy Spirit, who mediates and preserves for us the living
faith, retains contact with the Son and the Father. It is, to
a certain extent, our responsibility to see that he finds in
our spirit a dwelling place for his triune life. Only the
Holy Spirit of the Trinity can give our spirit a share in
eternal life. Just as the incarnate Son placed himself
completely at our disposal, even to death on the Cross,
so the Holy Spirit is at the disposal of the believer, to

keep alive in him the call bestowed on him by the Spirit and to make the word of God daily audible in him. It is this word that must become the law of life for one in an ecclesial state so that, by means of his Christian life, he can, in his own way, cause the word to become flesh anew and thus contribute to the living continuance of Christ and the Church throughout the ages.

In One's Surroundings

It is necessary to consider here both the surroundings in which an individual lived before his choice and those into which he entered by reason of it. Both must be affected by the Christian choice of a state of life, in relation to the new experiences of the one who chooses. There begins a new exchange that is conditioned by many factors: by the choice itself, by the way of life thus chosen, and even by the dissociation from such a way of life on the part of those who have made no choice. In one who has made his choice the old and new ways of life meet not only in the personal form for which he is responsible before God but also in an objective confrontation in which, as a person, he has only a small part to play. He has himself become a point of convergence.

Because one who enters a new state of life either completely dissociates himself from his former surroundings or establishes a kind of distance between himself and them, this environment loses a member who had belonged to it. The people in this environment feel deprived in some sense of what is theirs by right—and so they are. A breach has been made, and the question now is how it is to be filled. For a time, it can be filled by the astonishment of those in his surroundings that anyone should dare to break away, to take his leave, to refuse to let himself be shaped by his milieu but rather to choose in freedom. The breach can also be filled by quick forgetfulness. But one who is leaving his former acquaintances should see to it that the void thereby created continues to raise the same questions that led him to his choice. It lies in the logic of his choice that he leaves the state of nonchoice not only for his own advantage, in order to enter the state he has chosen, but also in order to convince those still in the state of nonchoice of the rightness and necessity of a genuine choice. The Son of God did not become man only for the one who has chosen, but for all. In like manner, the call addressed personally to the Christian is intended also for all Christians and establishes a relationship between him and them. Many persons slip from their old surroundings into marriage of whom it cannot be said with certainty that they have really chosen marriage. It is an indication that someone has made a Christian choice in favor of marriage if he has an urge to present the Christian state of marriage in a new light to all around him: not only to the many Christians who have not rightly understood the ecclesial quality of their marriages but also to those who have never seriously explored the question of marriage as a Christian state of life. He wants to help demonstrate the sanctity of marriage. He knows that he himself will experience things in his chosen marriage that will be radiantly eucharistic and apostolic in character. The same is true in even greater measure of the other two states of life.

When it was time for a genuine choice, that choice was made in prayer, either during or outside the Spiritual

Exercises. In the normal course of events, this time which is characterized by a serious, intimate standing of the soul before God included from the start a consideration of the Church and the community. The life eventually chosen reveals itself as the right one by its fruitfulness for the neighbor, and neighbors in this context are always those whose lives one has thus far shared. The social implications of someone's choice must be evident not just to him but also to his acquaintances. The choice should not be regarded as a decision commendable in itself but fruitful and beneficial only for him who makes it. The individual has become the exponent of an ecclesial concept, of God's claim upon those who live in the Church. Certainly he has made his choice as a person and was perhaps never so totally a person as in the making of it. But with his choice he has entered into the anonymity of a particular state of life and has become its commissioned representative. He must direct the attention of his acquaintances less to his personal way than to his chosen state, which he must recommend by his existence to those who have not yet made their choice.

Christ bestowed his word on us in such a way that it never loses its vital efficacy. Everything that is done in his name and in the name of his word shares in the power of his vitality. If the word is so efficacious in a given individual that it leads him to choose a state of life and so to dissociate himself from his former life of nonchoosing, it will also be powerful enough to exert its influence as word beyond the person of that individual: to act on his acquaintances, to rouse them and to effect in them that for which the individual's departure is but the outward occasion. Every leave-taking causes uneasiness in those who are left behind. In like manner, every arrival in a state of life should create uneasiness in those who believe they have already arrived in it—for instance, the arrival of a novice in a cloister. This uneasiness is less plainly visible in the married state because that state is represented before God more by the sum total of all married people than by an individual couple. The latter will, it is true, have experienced all the uneasiness of becoming, but it will then join the vast number of more or less unknown couples who have little part in such becoming. The emotional stress of the choice and of beginning a family, on the other hand, will awaken a much deeper response in the married couple—all the more because their social unit is so small. An analogous situation ought to exist in the other states of life: those who have been longer in a particular state should begin again in spirit with the arrival of every aspirant and, in his entrance into the community, should relive their own entrance. Naturally, a novice should not be made to feel that the order has been awaiting his arrival and that his coming is a special event. It is rather the objectivity of the word of God, the strength of which is made manifest even in the case of the novice, that is of value for those who are already members of the community. He is but the instrument of all this, as his state of life persistently demands that he be. It is not the account of his doubts and victories that is important but the fact that one can believe anew in the power of the word that has been victorious even in such a one as he.

With the birth of a new child there is, in every family, a shifting of balances that recalls earlier shifts, the first of which took place with the sealing of the marriage bond.

In marriage everything is new. Then the first child comes and everything is new all over again—and so it is with the birth of each child. In marriage, the ability to renew and to arouse from slumber arises from its own fruitfulness, which in turn is founded on the antecedent fruitfulness of the decision to marry, the Christian preparation for marriage, the time of engagement and the marriage itself. One's extended family and one's acquaintances also have their share in these events, but with them the sphere of the events' effect is, from a human point of view, essentially complete. The effect of events is very different in the case of the evangelical state because it in some sense comprehends the whole order— not by such clearly outlined events as mark the lives of married persons, but in a way that surpasses empirical experience while allowing the individual religious to participate: in the sphere of the rule inspired by the Holy Spirit and of the way the order appears before God, but especially in the sphere in which the Son, founding the Church, stands before the Father. The force of events is much more efficacious and far-reaching in the evangelical state because it is, as it were, immediately taken by God to be passed on to those who have preserved a memory of these events. From without, the event is not particularly striking—it is not a question of major feasts with recognizable graces, the profession of vows or ordination to the priesthood; the activity is entirely in the depths of God's being, in that place where the Father sends the Son and where the mission of the Church is already contained in the mission of the Son. In each new choice by which an individual consecrates his life to the following of the Son, the Son's word lives anew on earth and the Incarnation is realized anew in the Church and especially in the religious order. It would be completely insufficient to equate this process with the ordinary effects of prayer. In every perfect decision to follow the Son, the Son demonstrates anew to the Father that the Father's will is done on earth as it is in heaven, that his kingdom is coming and that there are persons who place their lives at the disposal of this kingdom. It is this that has its effect on the order and on the Church.

***

Also to be considered are the individual's former school-mates, contemporaries and friends. Many of them should also be making the choice of a state of life, and they should be made newly aware of this fact and of its claim upon them by the choice that has been made by one of their number. There are others for whom it is too late to make such a choice; but they, too, should experience a stimulus they can incorporate into their life of prayer and can transfer from there to their daily lives. Perhaps they are already numbered among those who remained stationary; perhaps they failed to hear the Lord's call. But Christian hope is not for that reason denied them— the hope that God will have mercy on them and will make the best of their situation. It is important that they do not begin, by reason of the decision and attitude of the person who has made his choice, to regard themselves as outcasts, as inferior, as those for whom no meaningful way remains open. And, if perhaps they come to realize that it would have been better if they had made a choice, they will seek to influence in this respect others for whom it is not too late.

One choosing a state of life should show gratitude to

his family. They have shared in his choice at least to the extent of not putting obstacles in the way of his making it and have probably also given it their positive support by means of education and innumerable influences. If the individual is planning to enter a religious order, he will attempt, by his inner equanimity and openness, to make those who remain behind more familiar with the spirit of the life in the order he has chosen. His entrance into religious life means a sacrifice for his family, and it should be fruitful for them. They should feel that they have a share in the sacrifice he makes by entering, should even learn to pray for the religious order he has chosen and, for the future, to preserve their bond with him through prayer. They should have a certain interest in the life of the order, but without an excessive curiosity that would seek to ferret out all its internal procedures. Their prayer life should expand by reason of the new attitudes and concerns that are opened to them. Their Catholic world view in general should be broadened and intensified. Despite the individual's grateful love for his family, his parting from them is nevertheless a total one. His family will not be able henceforth to share in or to influence the destiny of the one who has left them. The renunciation is to be borne as such. The fact that those he leaves share in a hidden way in the grace of his vocation is a living truth of faith, but it cannot be interpreted in terms of our everyday life. A certain harmless effusiveness in Saint Thérèse of Lisieux's relationship with her family is not to be regarded as exemplary in this respect.

Something analogous is true in the case of those who marry. They, too, take leave of their families. Granted, they will see their dear ones more often, but their thoughts must be centered now around their new life.

This requires discretion on the part of the family and, on the part of the young married couple, a certain determination that wards off interference. This is true even if their parents' home was a model Christian one. Marriage also includes renunciation on both sides. Young persons who want to establish their own family must be allowed to assume their own responsibility.

For the person concerned, the problem can become a difficult one, for there seems to be a conflict of duties. He does not see how he can spare those he loves the pain of parting. The solution is not to look upon the end of his former way of life and the beginning of his new one as a kind of destiny before which all heads must bow, but rather to regard it as a free, creative action in which everyone, including the family and one's other acquaintances, share in a Christian manner. In this, the ecclesial character of the life of faith must show itself: what is realized in the one who departs and those who remain behind is a piece of the living Church in her living order of the states of life. Despite all personal suffering and perhaps unanswered questions, all those in the ecclesial sphere must seek to establish a mutual balance. Perhaps the one who has chosen to enter the religious life or to become a priest will be called upon later to speak and preach about marriage. He should be able to do so from a balanced perspective whose foundations were laid in his youth and at the time of his entrance into the novitiate or seminary. The Lord himself established this relationship when, with the same objective relationship and the same subjective problems of painful separation and deeper continuity, he built the New Testament on the foundation of the Old Testament. He uses the Old Testament as a point of departure, doing justice to it and letting it become fruitful in the New Testament beyond its every expectation, yet he demands of his followers a very clearcut decision; he brooks no compromise, and he turns away his relatives, and even his Mother, when they personify "flesh and blood" for him. In the relationship of the two Testaments, the Son has proclaimed firmly and forever the laws that govern the choice of a state of life. And behind his lawmaking stands his own fixity of purpose in his Incarnation: he became man without denying his divinity, yet "he did not consider it necessary to cling" to his divinity; he left it in the Father's care and lived resolutely as man without constantly complaining that heaven was a more beautiful and pleasant place than earth.

In the Church

The chosen state is an ecclesial state. In it are certain sacraments or forms that are reserved for this particular state. But it also possesses what is common to all the states. As an institution, the Church participates constantly in the ecclesial states that exist within her. She does so above all by approving them and establishing the criteria for their existence: the sacraments and the manner in which they are to be administered and received, the regulation of the vows and the other obligations and duties of the evangelical life, and much else that belongs to the Church as a whole and which she places at the disposal of those in the states of life. The Church respects the existence and nature of each individual state in its particularity as well as the freedom of those who belong to it, the freedom which the state as such must preserve if it is to administer those things that have been entrusted to it and those it has undertaken on its own initiative, subject only to the "nihil obstat" of the Church.

There are many gradations in the relationship of the states of life to the Church: from the clearly explicit to the discreetly suggested, from the strictly required to the merely desirable or even merely permitted. Thus for the conduct of Christian marriage there are inexorable commands and prohibitions, then precautions, directives and recommendations, and finally a variety of matters that are left to the judgment of the individual. The Church must always be the soil in which the seed of the state of life is to grow; but there are areas in which it gives the sowers freedom to sow as they will and to cultivate what they have sown.

It is also true that the Church as an organization has only a limited range of contact with the world. This contact can be all the more strongly fostered by those in the states of life. One might argue that the most contemplative and withdrawn order has a more objective and true conception of the real world than does the institutional Church as such. It follows that the states of life must pass on to the Church, of which they are, as it were, the agents for this purpose, the experiences they glean from the circumstances and tendencies of the modern world. As an institution and "machine", the Church has, above all, the obligation to defend herself and her continued existence in the world. To this end she strives for permanency. The turbulent elements in the Church are the states of life; they are constantly bringing forth new things in the Church and are also constantly in need of her renewed support. Even if everything in the Church and the states of life were perfectly ordered, she would nevertheless still have the task not only of making what she receives from the states of life fruitful for the Church as a whole but also of asserting and affirming herself and her permanent structure amid all the innovative strivings of the states of life. In a certain sense, the Church is the "body" and the states of life are the "soul", and between them are circulation, exchange and life. The life of the spirit must, as always, be considerate of the body, but the life of the body must not suffocate the spirit. Both are necessary if resistance from both sides is to be reduced to a minimum and they are to prove fruitful. Each is interested in the well-being of the other because they are, by their nature, ordered to one another and together form a whole. The states of life are dependent on the Church, just as the Church needs the states of life.

When Paul asserts that Christ is the head of the Church just as husband is the head of the wife, the comparison is indicative of much in the relationship of the Church both to her communities and to the ecclesial states of life. The allusion to Christ as head of the Church gives the image its maximum frame of reference; the allusion to the husband as head of the wife gives it its minimum frame of reference. Between the two lies the whole ecclesial order. We might regard the Church as the head, the states of life as her members. But in doing so we must not forget that the members not only have each their own idea but are, on the whole, more concrete and have a more personal contact with God. Seen thus, the Church would be the body. But whatever interpretation we accept, the important thing is their reciprocal orientation, their mutual relationship. Hence someone who undertakes any work within the Church (for example, the writing of a book about spiritual matters) must be at once head and member: he must ponder and plan as a free intelligent spirit, yet he must at the same time submit his intellect, his freedom and his plans to God and let himself be guided and influenced by him. Since time began, God has had but one purpose in mind: to incorporate us into his plans so that, in the instant in which we are wholly incorporated, he may set us free again. He binds us and looses us. He sets our feet on the right path only to release us again. And should I write this book, God will indeed show me the direction that leads to himself, and in that same instant I must look in the other direction. I cannot speak of his greatness if I do not know our smallness. Both lines converge in my stand before God: his greatness reveals itself in our human insufficiency. Something similar exists between the Church and the states of life; the Christian is permitted to live at the point where the two meet, just as he also lives at the meeting-point between the world he lived in before his choice and the state of life he has chosen. And that is perhaps the greatest mystery of the Christian life: that it is a meeting-point, source, beginning and end which are fruitfully united.

In one sense, all of us—whether Church or state of life or individual—are related to one another as pupils and teachers. The teacher assigns a task that seems clear to him; the pupil tries again and again to complete it but is unable to do so. He tries to do what he is supposed to do. If he cannot, then the teacher will ask himself if he has presented the task correctly, that is, if he has done what he is supposed to do. He will make the task easier, which may be more difficult for him to do. Thus there is always a relationship of reciprocal adaptation and accommodation: between man and the Church, between man and the state of life, between the Church and the state of life, between Christ and the Church, and finally in Christ himself, as the "order of salvation", between God and man. The pupil feels humiliated before the teacher if he keeps doing the work wrong. But the teacher is humiliated when he realizes he has not explained it well. This humiliation, which can be more painful for the teacher than for the pupil, is what the individual often experiences in relation to his state of life. It also makes itself felt in the relationship of the state of life to the Church and of the Church to the state of life because it is, in the last analysis, the embarrassment inherent in man's distance from God and in his realization of that distance.

***

The guiding principle of the one who has made his choice is not chiefly the choice itself, but the call. The Lord has called him, and he has heard and answered the call. Now the call continues to live in him and demands his constant response. In the beginning, he had to make a choice in order to answer. Now he is in the condition of having chosen; he cannot repeat his choice. If he were to make it an object of meditation, he would be contemplating his own achievement. The call is different; it is not a *fait accompli*, nor can his answer be such. Both before and after his choice, the call continues to be active and urgent. In the beginning, it was a call to a state of life; now it signifies his mission within that state. But this happens always in the context of the Lord's call, always precisely *as* the Lord's call. It is less important that the individual regard his mission as related to his state of life than that he experience it as God's call to him at this particular moment. His state of life is only the framework within which God calls him. He should hear that call by which his mission is perhaps specifically defined and by which he is shown the path he must follow to accomplish it, and which he should always assume that he has not yet sufficiently answered. If he were to grow accustomed to equating God's call with the ordinary requirements of his state of life, he would become deaf to God; he would no longer have a personal relationship with God but only the relationship intrinsic to his state of life.

This is true also in cases where a personal decision has led the individual to adapt himself to a markedly objective and anonymous rule: in the religious state. The rule is not God, nor is God the rule. Within the framework of the rule, the person of living faith must be at pains to hear God's personal and unremitting call to him. Certainly he hears the call now with the ears of one who has chosen, but that means that his state of life bestows on him certain new capabilities by virtue of which he hears the call in a new way. He, the hearer, has become a different person. His state of life acts upon him, shaping and changing him; his whole attitude is altered. God can say to him now things he would not previously have been able to hear. New worlds open up to him. As a result of having made his choice and having persevered in it, he acquires a new certainty. This gift was inherent in his choice and now reveals its power. At first he was overwhelmed by the thought that God had chosen to entrust such a responsible mission to one as incapable and weak as he. He evaluated himself and had some notion of his limited capabilities. If it had been up to him, he would have narrowed the framework of his calling. For his part he would have been ready to follow God, but, for the sake of the fidelity required of him, he would have considered it more prudent not to go so far. Now that he has consecrated himself to God, wings carry him as they do the bird that leaves the nest for the first time and gradually acquires the habit and certainty of flying.

Others have never taken this risk and have remained in the first stage of self-evaluation. They have, perhaps, remained unmarried because they wanted to serve God; but because they did not see the need for total sacrifice, because they did not have the grace to give themselves once and for all, they could not entrust everything to grace. While holding fast to their self-evaluation, they also had at some point to evaluate the power of grace. They believe there is a certain equivalence between their present mode of existence and grace; they trust this equivalence because it seems to promise nothing unforeseen or, at most, only small surprises. "If I promise little, I am better able to keep my promise": this rule may be valid on the natural level, but it will be rejected by those who entrust themselves to grace. If someone has given himself totally in his choice, he suddenly realizes that the call never ceases to grow but grace grows with it— for God's voice is the voice of grace—and that one's strengths, the wings God has given one, grow even as the demand grows.

One who has answered God's call may have to live a long time in dryness, in spiritual darkness. But he must not for that reason lose his certainty of being on the path indicated by the call. It is not possible for someone to answer God's call and for God not to hear his answer. He has only to persevere in the life to which he has been called and do everything, prayer and actions, in the certainty of having been called. Whatever he does has, by reason of the answer he has given, a deeper meaning than before, and he is also assured of a more unconditional protection than before. This is not something he has earned. He lives under the law of the grace that follows upon the answer he has given.

The Church, too, is seen in a new light from the perspective of life according to the call. Every state offers its own particular perspective and an outlook different from that of any other state or of the individual who has chosen no state. The landscape of God and his Church presents itself differently. Different questions reveal their urgency; different solutions must be found. And there is an inner necessity to concern oneself with what is shown. If someone makes an excursion into the mountains and is able to enjoy from the summit a view so beautiful that it makes all his effort seem worthwhile, it would be foolish of him to immerse himself in a book about architecture or about the beauties to be found in the depths of the ocean. . . .

The relationship between God and the Church, between the Bridegroom and the Bride, is unquestionably a stable and permanent one. But its absoluteness lies above all in God and in God's own choice. He chose to found a Church; this choice had its place in his decision to become man. Revelation makes known to us a great number of God's choices that seem to be juxtaposed but are in reality all contained in and form various aspects of his one choice to redeem the world and allow it to participate in the divine life. All the acts performed by the Son on earth have their origin in this one choice, are linked to and united with it and proceed necessarily from it. When, therefore, we have tasks to accomplish in our state of life within the Church, we can be certain— if we persevere in God's call—that our choices are encompassed by the framework of our original choice, which was itself contained in the Lord's choice. Whatever in our actions may strike us as questionable, whatever in our offer of ourselves may seem to have a fortuitous and relative character, comes from the fact that we are human and sinful and that our actions can never be the Lord's actions. Nevertheless, we can always live at the center, the axis, of God's choice. Both belong together; they are simply two different aspects of the "ever-more" of God's nature.

No one can do all that is to be done. He must do what he can. Let us suppose I am the only surgeon after a battle and there are a thousand wounded to be treated: wherever I begin, most of them will come to grief. I can seek out the most urgent cases, but I must not lose too much time in reaching a decision; the main thing is to do something. This is the position of everyone in the Church, where there is such a superfluity of work to be done that one hardly knows where to begin. No single individual is the whole Church. Each takes the place to which he has been called and tries to understand and do his assigned tasks from this place. All places in the world—but also in the Church—offer different perspectives.

V

Difficulties

Difficulties with Regard to Understanding and Being Understood

In the process of choice—even in the most favorable circumstances, the humblest submission to the call—there is an immediately observable gap between the greatness of the call and the smallness of man's answer. It is man who says Yes. His Yes is a human Yes, depending for its existence on the Mother's Yes to the angel and on the service of the human Mary to her divine Son. It is a Yes at once enveloped and assimilated by Christian grace. Nevertheless, perhaps precisely because it is borne by grace, it splits open the distance between God and man, between call and answer, between demand and possible compliance. Even the most tranquil Yes-sayer knows a certain fear: is it really he and not someone else who has been designated and chosen? His "Yes—why not?" contains a trace of astonishment and hesitancy that reflects the Mother's astonishment and her question: "How shall this be, for I know not man?" The angel's answer may or may not be plainly heard, but it is unquestionably given, though never in a form comprehensible to nature alone; for only in faith does man know that he is living in grace. As long as he lives on earth he will never cease to experience the traces and consequences of original sin, and hence can never be certain of not falling into sin. He is not permitted to rest comfortably in a human certainty that would lead only to pride and presumption. For the most part, he understands that the call is meant for him, yet he never completely understands that it is. He utters his assent knowing full well that only grace can assure his worth and perseverance before God. His gift is contingent upon and supported by God's gift. This combination of understanding and nonunderstanding accompanies him into the state of life he has chosen. Even if he attains to the highest office and dignity, he will continue to regard himself as one who has entered this state through some oversight that there is no further opportunity to clarify or reconsider and that consequently will be with him until the end. The feeling that already characterized the relationship between the Lord's call and his own answer to it is later repeated in his state of life. If he has chosen the religious life, he will never completely understand certain aspects of it because the rule and spirit of the congregation, insofar as they have remained living, always bear witness to the spirit of the saint who gave them their initial impulse and who lived in the intimacy of the Holy Spirit—a spirit that is accessible only indirectly to the saint's disciples. The nature of the saints, their work and the legacy they have left us, is comprehensible up to a certain point. Beyond that point, the saints are unfathomable to us. If it were not so, they would not be the disciples and elect of the Son, whose work of interpreting God, a work that is comprehensible to all the faithful, is inextricably rooted in the mystery of the triune life. In fact, the more we understand this, the more the Son—and, in imitation of him, the saint—reveals it to us, the greater the incomprehensible appears to us, so that the relation between the comprehensible and the incomprehensible will never resolve itself in our favor.

We find this exemplified in the regulation of daily work by minute rules that are meaningful only when all of them refer to the Lord. But not directly, for the Son is infinitely superior to our small works; we must not narrow our concept of him to the format of individual prescriptions of the rule. We must allow the Lord his greatness and the rule its concreteness, and we must not attempt to fit them into a manageable system. To attempt seriously to do so would mean a failure to realize that we can never so manipulate the Lord and his presence in the Church that he will fit into our small syntheses.

Or, to take another example, a priest has many penitents. He would like to spend much time in counseling them, but, because of their great number, he must content himself with a somewhat summary and average performance of his duty. This irks him. He does not understand why it must be so, for it seems to him to border on a desecration of the sacrament. But he reminds himself again of Christ's preaching—how Christ spoke to great crowds of people and then dismissed them, even hid himself from them and allowed others to return home unconverted.

Or an individual has entered upon a good Christian marriage. Then difficulties arise that, with the best will in the world, he is unable to overcome. Perhaps he is unable to satisfy both his wife and his children because their demands are different and even antithetical. He does not fully understand his situation; he cannot cope with it. Whatever he does seems but a half measure. This insufficiency, which is present in every state of life, is often hard to bear. And it is all the harder if the individual sees no way of dealing with it, yet must say to himself that he has gotten into this situation by reason of an honest assent to God.

***

One who has lived in the religious state for a long time and has perhaps lost some of his inner dynamism begins, after a while, to judge the people around him from the standpoint of his own tepidity. We would have to be more or less like him for him to feel any affinity with us. But because his life and his understanding are no longer drawn from the living center, his nonunderstanding is, in point of fact, the basis of what he regards as understanding.

The vitality of the Son reveals itself in his ability to understand us, even though we are different from him, in terms of what he is himself. As Son, he does the will of the Father; he joins his will to that of the Father in such a way that he lives from the Father's life, possesses it in himself and bears witness to it—a living, ever-growing witness that has its deepest foundation in the fact that the Son allows himself to be generated from all eternity by the Father and that, consequently, the Father, in generating the Son from all eternity, also manifests and bears witness to himself. Not only does the Son bear witness to the Father but, in the testimony of the Son, the Father bears witness to the Son inasmuch as he generates the Son and testifies to this action, which takes place wholly within the Godhead, by means of the Son's mission in the world. The eternal vitality of God's inner life bears witness to itself in the word of the Son; it reveals itself to the world and, in this revelation, continues to be essentially present. If the witness of the Son is a revelation of the one generated, it is so because the Son himself is a revelation of the one who generates. That is the absolute vitality of the Son, who completely encompasses and envelops our life and therefore understands us thoroughly, even in those things in which we are different from him. Correspondingly, the vitality received from the source—and, in the last analysis, from the state of being generated from the Father by grace together with the Son—is the prerequisite for understanding the states of life. An individual who no longer understands his religious order shows by this fact that he no longer allows himself to be continually generated from the supernatural spirit of that order, but rather regards himself as one who generates the order and renders the order a service simply by belonging to it. If he should happen to be responsible for his fellow religious or for the novices, he will give to the rules that he explains and interprets the meaning which his atrophy allows him to give. Practically, they will have become for him a dead letter and no longer the expression of the Word that issues perpetually and in living fashion from the Father—the Word that is the Son. Nor will he be able to understand how a fellow religious can live with a fresh assent in the vitality of God and his perceptible call and how the call he hears leads him back again and again to the Word that calls, that makes all things the expression for him of God's present will, that envelops him in a life which is formed by the religious order, but whose content perpetually radiates and flows from God.

As Catholics, we live in the Son's word as it comes to us from the gospel. But this word that is spoken to us and that has validity for us has validity also for the Church as a whole and for all mankind as it stands in need of redemption. In order that this validity of the word for the rest of mankind may also be proclaimed and known in the circle of our limited receptivity, Christ has established in his Church the states of life that compel those who live in them to keep their horizons open from the beginning to that which is more than personal. The states of life form a field of tension that serves as mediator between individuals and the Church as a whole with her relationship to the world: as mediator because the states of life, though they constitute the whole life-form of the individual, belong wholly also to the structure of the Church. (It is possible to observe the opposite of this in Protestantism, where the individual's attempt to take a position with regard to the Word of God that is Christ that does justice to the objectivity of the relationship of Christ to his Church repeatedly founders.) The ecclesial state is a framework within a framework, the humanly possible within the impossible. The Lord himself accomplishes for us whatever in his demands is beyond our ability to accomplish, leaving us what we are to accomplish in a framework that is less tautly drawn and, therefore, adapted to our weakness. The individual who commits himself to follow Christ in the evangelical state is perhaps best aware of this: he professes an idea of the Lord, a very concretely conceived plan of redemption, and knows, in the process, that it is more a case of his being borne by the Lord than of his helping to bear the Lord's burden. Indeed, he not only knows that he is borne by the Lord's grace; he also feels that it is the Lord himself who accomplishes the crucial, living dedication of self, the boundless surrender to the divine fire, thus allowing his servant to lead a somehow sheltered life in his chosen state. In consequence, the state of life always has about it an aura of divine kindness, of a game with rules of its own in which God himself takes part. This, too, is something that is lacking to the Protestant, who always stands alone before the whole task, who has only both ends—"at once a sinner and justified"—in his hands without being able to bring them together, and who does not see how he can really be adequate to the greatness of what is required of him. If we take them seriously, the states of life in the Catholic Church relieve the struggling individual of concern as to whether he can accomplish something by his own effort. Whatever he accomplishes, it is the state that acts through him as he acts through the state, thus making the division of labor in the Catholic sphere a much more general and anonymous one. Most of the questions about the relationship of grace and merit can be answered only by reference to the states themselves. There is merit in cooperating with grace; yet the individual who reflects upon his personal merit will lose it. If, on the other hand, he is fully aware that grace and achievement have come to him because he belongs to and is a representative of a state of life, he will have no hesitancy in ascribing to that state whatever merit he may seem to have accumulated. His state of life is, for him, a point of exchange at which the personal element acquires a social and comfortably anonymous visage. Nor is this effectiveness proper only to his own state; all the states of life exist for one another and advance the well-being of one another by prayer and Christian life.

Life in the Christian states thus transcends the ego and its consciousness. What once appeared to be a divine concession—namely, that our consciousness is not expected to be coextensive with God's absolute demand—now appears as a divine help for rising above our subjectivity, for holding ourselves open, through the medium of our state of life, to God's objective demand. We entrust ourselves to the superior way of life, but it constantly sets us back on our own feet. The virgin does not, perhaps, "understand" what happens to her on her wedding night; but the birth of the child casts a retrospective light onto that first experience. What continues to be incomprehensible in the state of life should always be the origin of life to come and should let itself be justified by its fruit.

***

The fact that an individual has chosen a state of life is a constant reminder to him of the incomparably personal act he posited in making his choice and in all the struggles and reflections associated with it. Even when two persons make the same choice, their choice does not place them on the same level. The paths they have hitherto followed and the personal coloring of their choice will forever distinguish them. Nevertheless, the personal element will henceforth be joined to the objective ideal of the chosen state. And the way in which the two are joined can also be a personal one and a source of difficulties and misunderstandings among members of the same state. For example, one who has recently entered the religious life will understand this tension differently than does a senior member of the community who has formed his opinion gradually over a number of years. He has a particular concept of the state of life and of his own nature as well as of the relationship between the two. But this whole range of concepts will be perceived differently by his fellow religious. The newcomer also feels somehow that he is not understood. The attitude of the older members toward the life of the community is not the same as his: could he have been deceived when he made his choice with a particular ideal in mind? And even though he did, at the time, try to foresee possible disappointments, these disappointments are different from what he anticipated. He understands clearly that the state of life will inevitably change those who enter it. But it is difficult for him to understand why it has not changed them in a different, more fundamental manner.

In the married state, the fact of being in love helps to smooth and lighten the difficulties of the first period, especially if it is based on genuine love and mutual compatibility. At first, perhaps, certain differences make themselves felt more strongly than one had anticipated; but if both partners have goodwill and are unselfish in their love, they will daily become more accustomed to one another. Married persons expect to be helped less by their state of life than by their personal mutual effort to adapt to one another—an effort that is the more urgently needed the more their first romantic love begins to fade. In religious life, the state itself plays something of the role that infatuation and love play in marriage, and this is true even though one's relationship to one's state is not necessarily identical with one's relationship to God and need not develop along parallel lines. One's relationship to God, one's prayer, one's readiness for sacrifice receive their special character from the state without necessarily becoming for that reason more vital. There is a grace proper to the novitiate, but it would be incorrect to say that the question of whether or not one is understood is an acute one at this time. The novitiate is a preliminary stage, not yet the full religious state. Also to be considered is the novice's personal relationship with the master of novices, their "compatibility". The novice master, to a great extent, represents the order for the novice, more than is objectively the case.

In marriage, the child is a strong personal confirmation of the parents' choice as well as of their mutual understanding. From the perspective of the child, the father's masculine nature and the mother's feminine one become more comprehensible even to the parents. In the religious state, the moment of fruitfulness is more distant; one's sacrifice cannot be understood in such a natural frame of reference. The mystery of this state is so close to the mystery of the Lord's Incarnation that the understanding of it cannot go beyond certain limits.

The priesthood stands between the other two states in this respect as well, since it places the emphasis neither on understanding, as does the married state, nor on the absence of understanding, as does the religious state. It is situated in the flux between "world" and "nonworld". In the married state, the I–Thou relationship leads more and more deeply into the reality of the state of life; in the religious state, the rule molds the individual by its universal applicability; in the priesthood, the deciding factor is the sphere which is formed by the office, but which is to be understood neither as an I–Thou relationship nor as a rule. As a way of life, it is formed interiorly by two factors: the hierarchical aspect, with its responsibility for the word of God, its transmission to souls and its acceptance by them; and the administration of the sacraments, which gives the priestly life a kind of effervescence that stems from the mystery of the sacramental process. The life of the priest could have its living center in the mystery of the Holy Mass, with no possibility of finding its center of gravity in the personal element or in anything resembling a rule, because the mystery of transubstantiation encompasses and masters everything. Lived thus radically, it would be an existence in the mystery of the Incarnation of the Word, that is, entirely in process and event, not yet at the stage of becoming a permanent state of life. It would be an existence in a state of catalysis, in which neither the catalyst nor the substance acted upon reveals its full nature. But the hierarchical aspect of the priest's life would also have to be affected and defined by this existence in process and event. Because life in the sacramental process is not sufficient to create the form of a state of life, it cannot be allowed to undertake, by itself, the founding of a state of life. For such a course would lead quickly to alienation and obduracy, to the detriment of both person and office. Considered solely in itself, the sacramental aspect cannot be the foundation of a state of life because no community life can be formed out of it alone. After being ordained priests, the Apostles received the Body of the Lord at the Last Supper and drank his Blood. And after the Lord's Ascension into heaven, they continued to live a communal life in the breaking of bread, which was, for them, a reminder of the Cross. But the breaking of bread could not of itself shape their concrete life in community: they added to it the elements of the evangelical life. Human life has a breadth and a structure that cannot be derived from pure event. That is why there exists no purely priestly community; the individual priest possesses a kind of self-reliance that the other states do not bestow in equal measure. He stands on his own. He is not actually responsible for the priest of a neighboring community (as the married man may be responsible for other marriages or the religious for his fellow religious), except, of course, insofar as it is required of him by the bond of love of neighbor. For that reason, the problem of "understanding and nonunderstanding" does not even arise for him. If the priest seeks a state of life that will embrace his whole human existence, he will look for it in one of the other two states. And if he finds his life and its justification in being in a third state between these two, it is because of the provisional character of the whole earthly order, in which even the other states do not fully accomplish what they are supposed to accomplish and are in constant need of a catalyst to function between them, in somewhat the same way as the love between husband and wife is kept alive by the child that is a seed and a becoming between the two who already exist. That is why confession is also entrusted to the priest. If Christ's death on the Cross had transformed us immediately into what the Father wanted us to be, we would have no need of confession. Confession is also an event: the presence of redemption on the Cross for the sinner who, by confession and absolution, puts off the old man and clothes himself with the new. From this perspective, the disciples' life with the Lord was a life of constant confession. The priesthood in the Church helps the other two states, which so easily install themselves in permanency, to enter into the redeemed life anew through the sacraments. Thus the insufficiency of two of the states justifies the existence of the third.

Difficulties with Regard to Vitality and Fidelity

The disciples who followed the Lord's call scarcely knew what they were doing. They moved from one surprise to another; they learned to know him and to understand his teaching; their attitude was constantly being formed and improved by his. It was a life among men in which one was master and the rest followed, and the master was open, candid, unchangeable. Whatever in his teaching was difficult to understand was illuminated and animated not only by his explanation of it but also by his Person. His word could be harsh, blunt, almost unacceptable; he did the opposite of what anyone else might have done in his place. But however he showed himself, his disciples knew, or at least had an intimation, that he was in all respects the truth and the life. He was the Son of God, who opened to them the way to the Father. And as long as he was present among them, it was not difficult to follow him in the vitality and fidelity of their first call.

In the later ages of the Church, there were also persons filled with grace for whom the first call to discipleship and their response to it remained as fresh as if they had thereby entered into the circle of the Apostles. In most cases, however, the continued vitality of the call in the life of the one called is explicitly made dependent upon his cooperation. It is expected of him that he not become so accustomed to the life he has chosen that he becomes indifferent to it, but that he persevere in the attitude of the Apostles, for whom the daily intercourse with the Lord was a daily source of new wonder. The most important means to this end is contemplative prayer. If Christians succumb to the danger of understanding their relationship to God, not from the perspective of divine truth, but from that of their fellowmen or of the letter of their rule or of their plan of action, they have fallen away from the living center. Like the Apostles, they should not distance themselves from the call by so much as a step. For the living Lord brooks no substitute; nor is any state of life a substitute for him.

The disciples, who were called by the Lord and of whom it is said that they followed him, lived in his call. They entered into the reality of this call. The call was so constituted that it set them in motion and maintained them in it. Discipleship is the consequence of the call, and the life of discipleship is the consequence of the Lord's life. At no time—not even after the Ascension of the Lord—can the life of an Apostle be understood in terms of itself alone. Even John in his old age, when he had outlived all the others, can be understood only as one who lived in the obedience and love of the Lord. Should anyone attempt to cut the living cords that bind him to the Lord, his life will no longer be meaningful. So it is also in the life of the Christian. Whatever is not directly linked to the living call, whatever (in our opinion) has only an indirect or secondary relationship to it, has no meaning in the life of one who has been called.

Many a man acknowledges that his state of life has been determined by the Lord, but from the perspective of the call he is actually moving away from the Lord. He looks back on the time of his call as on a distant event. But that was not the purpose of the call. It was a call to a life that would daily understand the Lord better and follow him more closely. A call is always a new beginning, not a permanent quality. The fact that Holy Scripture is inspired means that the Holy Spirit is always living in it. This Spirit also has the power to present to us in a credible fashion the holiness of God in the events described and in the conduct of those who have been touched by it. God's holiness is a sudden fire that has the power to set a person aflame, today as well as in the time of Christ. Instead of realizing this, we have turned Holy Scripture into an infallible book about more or less interesting events that happened somewhere else a long time ago. But nothing of what happened then is concluded, for it is God's revelation, and God cannot be concluded. And a Christian state of life is not just an improved version of Adam's state, but a state of life in Christ.

A part of us is Adam until the call comes to us; a part of us is Old Testament until the moment when we choose and respond to God's call. Thereafter, we are the companions of the Lord, sharing the burden of his work: the work of redemption, which draws its strength from the essence of his life.

The Christian states of life are justified only as ecclesial states that make known to men throughout all ages the salvific will of the Son. There can be nothing more vital than this will, which is the perfect expression of the eternal will of the Father. Whoever speaks of the will of God speaks of God's action as it is happening, not of a pallid desire immured in a *fait accompli*. For the Son on earth that means the present and perpetual union of his will with that of the Father, the uninterrupted effort to realize the will of the Father. In the life of Christ, this daily and hourly renewal is the revelation of his generation by the Father now and from all eternity. He communicates something of this to his Bride, the Church, and to her states of life. Everyone who chooses a state of life shares, by the grace of that state, in this eternal generation. Far from freeing the individual from the obligation of personal striving, however, this grace renders him capable of it. Indeed, it draws him into the whole activity of the Trinity. Just as there is from all eternity in God the act of generation and its result, the living Son, so there must be in the life of the Christian this tension between *action and life*. He may not let himself be simply carried along by his chosen state and its vitality. That is not the fidelity that is expected of him. He must remain in the act and carry it out again and again so that this life can be affirmed, chosen and—to the extent that man is capable of it with the help of God's grace—brought forth in him. And this, again (as we have said above), is to take place in the living unity of tension between the person and his state of life.

Mary's assent to her Son had its source in her vitality. It was a word that corresponded perfectly to the fullness of the person she presently was, yet it lived, in antici-pation, from the life of the Son who would be conceived in her. The living Son who was to come corresponded exactly to her assent, and thus he was also the one who ensured that her assent would remain living and vital during the rest of her life. In someone who says Yes to the call to a state of life, person and state must mutually affirm each other if they are to remain living. And if the state is to say Yes, the one entering it must communicate to it so much of his own Yes that the state can produce the grace to ensure his fidelity. When the Lord's physical mother later became his spiritual Bride at the Cross, that which was efficacious in her self-surrender was confirmed. In founding the Church, the Son incorporated into her states of life not only something of the incomprehensible mystery of his generation in the Trinity but also something of the simple assent of the Mother who accompanied him throughout his life. If the Christian state of life were founded solely on the interior mysteries of God, weak man would not know how to meet its demands. But if Mary is present from the beginning, everything is easier. If my marriage seems unendurable, I may be tempted to say: "After all, God was never married." But when God says to me: "My Mother stood at the foot of the Cross", then I see that there have been human beings who did not turn away from the greatest difficulties. I do not for that reason have to be blind to the difficulties of my marriage any more than Mary was blind to the sacrifice of her Son. She stood by him with a vitality that had its source in him but was still her own; and what she suffered became part of the fullness of his sacrifice.

It is always possible for man to kill the word of God that is in him. By denying what the word is and what it means for him, he can, at any time, participate actively in the death sentence spoken by Pilate. But he who kills the word kills himself. He does so who fails to keep alive the word that has been entrusted to him. The awesome thing is that this truth applies from the moment in which man first hears the call of God. Until then, he had made no decision, for he was still in the process of growing up and was not yet mature. He was growing toward the word. But once he has made his choice—and even a choice refused is a kind of choice—he finds himself in a totally different position with regard to the word. It is no longer just exteriorly present for him; henceforth it is also to be in him. To have made my choice means to recognize that the word must be my center. If I do not want this, I kill the word. That has nothing to do with my attendance at sermons or my reading of Holy Scripture. It is a quality of the word in me that is determined by my Yes or No to God's call. The Lord, who is the Word, bestows himself on man and gives him the power to let the Lord live in his spirit or to die along with his spirit. For no one can preserve in his spirit a relationship to the divine Spirit who does not allow the divine Spirit to retain his trinitarian character, who does not allow the Word of God in man to preserve his divine, ever greater, more mysterious and thus more living significance. In no state of life can man deal conclusively with the Word. With his state of life he is welded into a unity in the Word and incorporated into this Word by the submission of his spirit to the Holy Spirit, who teaches him to do the will of the Father together with the Son.

When an individual comes to a decision and makes his choice, he must still have within him the full capacity for further development. He cannot choose from a position that is already so definitive for him that, in making his choice, he continues to be irrevocably the same as he was before because he knows precisely where he stands and who he is and is not willing to let himself be molded into something else. Many a person chooses his vocation on the basis of just such a prior decision, which obviates the possibility of any truly Christian choice: "*Because* I am so and not otherwise, I choose this vocation, which allows me to remain as I am and to become more and more so." One who chooses must be capable of being molded; this characteristic must, on the one hand, belong to the realm of what is possible for him and must, on the other hand, meet with no obstacle in the attitude of his will.

Many things will remain the same or will, at most,

only increase without changing in quality: for example, his love for his vocation and his fidelity. They will form the central core of his choice. Around them will be grouped his talent, his capabilities and his interests, which must develop according to the law of the center. Difficulties can arise here, for his vocation can suddenly lay claim to an aspect of his talent that he had hitherto regarded as unessential or only poorly developed, but that now illumines his nature in a new way, shifts balances and completely changes his image of his character. But if he was truly flexible in responding to God's call at the moment of his choice, he can be so also in the exercise of his vocation. This claim that suddenly challenges him in a different way is the living continuation of God's original call to him. In the living continuation of his choice, therefore, he must be flexible toward the word of God that now dwells within him; he must be confident that it can so mold him—and has, perhaps, already and without his knowing it, so molded him and guided him to maturity—that he is capable of meeting the present challenge.

Certainly there are difficulties. A person may be so sure of his choice that he relegates it to the past as a concluded event and no longer carries it out. Then one day the new man he deems himself to be can no longer find the old assent. Or a person may be so convinced of his talent and its duties that he expects the balance between them to remain forever unchanged. And now, though he is unaware of it, this apparently stationary balance has begun to shift; its inner proportions are changed. Or he may, at some previous time, have exerted a degree of control over himself and have continued to do so out of habit, but the situation has been altered by his gift of himself to the Lord; moments of recollection can present to him now a stranger in whom he no longer recognizes himself. Nevertheless, as a Christian he does not have the right to give up all self-knowledge and all consideration of self and to submit to the will of God in purely passive fashion by regarding himself as no more than a machine that is doing its duty.

The concept of *fidelity* is helpful here. Fidelity is a point of rest. Its characteristic is to remain, and to remain as it is. It establishes a relationship: to life, to one's decision, to God. But vitality is also necessary. One's decision, which was after all something vital, must not obstruct but rather encourage the capacity for development in the one making the choice. The act of deciding is not an intermittent growth toward maturity that goes so far and no further; it is the beginning of a genuine development that, to remain living, must repeatedly begin and establish itself anew. In the beginning is the call, which continues in the inspiration of the Holy Spirit and in the demands of one's vocation and of the Christian life, in both the narrowest and the broadest sense. Toward all this the Christian must not only not be insensible; he must become more and more open to it. Fidelity, then, is not just being at rest; it demands an inner awakening. It must itself be a living element of one's total vitality. Indeed, it must become vitality's living core, its fruitful seed.

This can be clarified by a glance at the sacramental life. In the reception of the sacraments there is a general, ecclesial fidelity proper to the Christian. But there is also, over and above this fidelity, a personal fidelity to God that finds expression in the will to let oneself be quickened again and again by the sacraments, to let objective grace act upon one. The child making his First Communion and the adult who receives Holy Communion frequently are the same person, the same Christian. The dedication once felt by the former is in essence the dedication felt today by the latter. The grace received in Holy Communion is also in essence the same, as is the demand of grace that one dedicate oneself again wholly to God. The differences that exist between the child and the adult, between the bud and the bloom of life, cannot break the continuity of fidelity, which is not a rigid identity but an identity of life. The youth who makes his choice must, in the act of choosing, reckon from the start with these two interrelated qualities: vitality and fidelity. He must undertake to desire to remain the person he was at the moment of his choice: one who heard the call of God in a living way and who determined to place his life now and forever at the service of God's word.

***

One who has made his choice has recognized that his life should have a meaning before God. In choosing, he does not squander his life but surrenders it. Even if he has no great opinion of himself or of his own importance, he may not henceforth regard this life, which now belongs to God, as a trifle. He has become answerable before God for its fruitfulness, actually for a twofold gift: for the gift of life that God made to him and for his gift of this life to God. The center of value is easily shifted: as a person, I am and remain unworthy before God; the worth lies in my vital, living life, in gratitude, in self-surrender. This thought moves the Christian to demand the best of himself even when he believes himself incapable of achieving this best by his own efforts. But the demand must remain because God's demands are always something absolute. The unworthiness of the person stands in contrast to the worthiness of his life. It is not to himself but to his life in the service of God that the Christian owes his best. That is the source of his fidelity.

But this correct fundamental concept can be the source of new difficulties. It is not impossible, on the one hand, for an individual to work out for himself in a kind of naive optimism a program for leading a life worthy of God, only to come face to face again and again with his unworthy and inept self, which is not ready for such a life. Nor is it impossible, on the other hand, for an individual to engage all his strength in the life thus planned while the self, who after all actually uttered the assent and promised the fidelity, is neglected and forgotten. The small efforts demanded by the daily practice of charity absorb all one's attention; the great effort initially made by the self is lost and overwhelmed in the fever of activity. Both approaches are wrong because they both fail to include and transform in any fruitful way the self and its free surrender. There is no life "after" the choice has been made that is not a living up to this choice. God required even Mary to renew her assent every day, and she knew from this that her assent was in truth a most incisive and life-giving word that could daily consecrate her whole existence anew to God. She shares this knowledge with us. Every prayer that looks contemplatively to Mary, every prayer that offers the

soul to the Holy Spirit, every genuine prayer is able—
and we should realize this!—to produce in us anew the
self-surrender that characterized our original choice. We
should give ourselves to God in the awareness that he has
the power to renew us at this and at every moment.

***

Like all the concepts that determine the meaning of one's
new life, the concepts of fidelity and vitality are intimately
associated, especially in the evangelical state, with the
transformation of the Christian life. They not only receive a new fullness and coloring; to a certain extent even
their content is changed. We must be prepared for constant surprises in this regard. For even if we knew, once
and for all, what constitutes fidelity, its development
would not coincide with that of the novice or the young
religious. Before and during his choice, the individual
may have thought he knew, with a degree of human
certainty, what constituted fidelity and vitality. He
believed he could discover them in himself and in his
fellowmen. After the choice, a new quantity comes to
the fore: God's fidelity and vitality. For God reveals
himself in a new way to one who surrenders himself to
him. Because of this revelation, human concepts change
to such a degree that they are henceforth always subject
to the divine influence. If the divine prototype is now the
norm, this means that man separates himself more and
more from his human life in order to live entirely by and
for the grace of God, to breathe with the rhythm of
God's breath. He lives and thinks in the atmosphere of
the divine word; what refreshes or strengthens him,
what allows him to exist, he draws from God's word.

Here, too, a difficulty may arise from the fact that one undertakes too much, that one tries too hard to comprehend the word and breath of God and so, in human terms, finds oneself breathless. One may engage all too vigorously in the struggle between the natural and the supernatural man. Objective tension and living unrest should not develop into subjective anxiety and a disturbance of the Christian balance; nor should rest in God become rest in oneself.

Difficulties with Regard to Faith, Hope and Love

Until someone has actually entered upon his chosen state of life, he has the feeling of being launched on a course of events that will end with his entrance, or perhaps even with his firm decision to enter, into that state. In retrospect, this course of events appears to have had as its goal his choice of a state of life and, in consequence, to shed light on many events of his earlier life that seem to have formed a closed system with the purpose of making him choose as he did.

Now, however, his decision opens to him the experience of a new life and consequently of a new faith, a new dedication, a new obedience. Many things that seemed to belong together must now separate completely in order to be joined together in a new way. The whole question of life in Christ, of his own personal existence in Christ, arises once again: not, this time, from the perspective of a vague, open-ended development, but with a push toward finality, since it is time now for aspirations to be realized. Before the choice, all relationships had a certain provisional character. The individual acted with a view to a possible, still uncertain choice. Now everything he does must be more planned, arising from the life he has chosen. Once he kept all avenues open. Before his marriage, he studied foreign languages, which would "be useful in any event"; he traveled to improve himself; he learned about men and relationships; but he did everything in the same purposely noncommittal manner. After his choice this lack of commitment is inappropriate, not only in external matters but above all in those internal ones that touch the core of his person and his state of life. Every word and teaching of the Lord resounds now with a new—because newly binding—significance. Formerly, when he pondered matters of faith, when he read or meditated or prayed, he was concerned above all to discover what a particular truth might mean for himself. The meaning retained its greatness and its many levels, but, depending on his mood, his frame of mind or his need, he was able to draw from it to some extent whatever appealed to him, enlightened him or helped him. After his choice, the meaning of God's word is always linked to the state he has chosen. Naturally there is a personal element in every meeting with the word. It is no longer free-floating, however, but is more closely linked to the chosen state of life; every word has a coloring that derives from that state. The believer cannot overlook this fact. On the contrary, he must so adapt himself to it that his future action on the basis of the word will also bear the mark of the state to which he belongs.

It is at this point that difficulties present themselves, for it is not easy suddenly to have to conduct oneself as the representative of a state of life and to do so not only outwardly, in the sense that one can learn and accustom oneself to use certain formal phrases, but also as inwardly as one is to one's own self, or even more, as inwardly as the word of God is the innermost law of one's life. The individual grows with the state of life he has chosen; he accepts its destiny as his own. If a member of the Church loses his faith, this fact has real, though not necessarily calculable, repercussions in the whole Church. It is one of those mysterious calculations that is known to God, and about which particularly apostolic souls are likely to be concerned. We know only the fact of the harm; we cannot measure its extent. Only when a larger number turn away from the Church or when an apostate begins to attack her violently can we see the possibility of serious harm to the Church. It is otherwise with a state of life. The harm an individual can do here is more serious because he chose this state of life, because at the age of decision he bound himself to it for life, because a state of life is considerably more circumscribed than the Church and its deficiencies more readily perceptible, and finally because the obligations of the state of life are more precisely defined, not only those of the states themselves but also those of the individual within his chosen state. It cannot be denied: the individual who has chosen a state of life is considered by the Church and the world to be the representative of his state. In him should be revealed what power to shape life and action is proper to that state. The other states look to him and hope to learn from him. He himself faces a series of tasks that seem to him at first to belong to the Church as a whole but that take on the specific character of his state of life once they have been entrusted to and accepted by him. As a result, any sign of tepidity or subjectivity, any lack of seriousness, has graver consequences.

In the Christian who is preparing to make his choice,

the universal Christian virtues of faith, hope and love usually acquire a personal stamp that enables him to approach the question of vocation, to study it, to reach a decision regarding it and to accept its consequences as an individual rather than as part of a crowd. At that time, everything possessed a certain misty beauty that he trusted with optimism and naiveté. Once he has entered upon a state of life, however, faith, hope and love acquire a largely predetermined character. They become now the faith, hope and love proper to that state, although the fact that they bear the mark of the state does not make them any less valid before God or the Church than was his earlier attitude, which had its source in personal enthusiasm.

But the transition can be difficult. One who comes to religious life after a good Catholic upbringing will be most aware of the change of atmosphere, from the personal to the objective atmosphere proper to the state. He will go through a period of alienation. His faith, hope and love, which have hitherto been unquestioningly ecclesial in character, will be affected and marked by this process. His faith was unconditionally Catholic and definitive in essence, but perhaps it was too general, too open-ended. After his choice, he must, therefore, find the strength to let himself be remolded to fit the needs of the Church as they relate to his new state. The basic truths of faith will, of course, remain unaltered, but the truths themselves will become, in their content, more significant than the person. They will determine his behavior, his work, his apostolate. The believer's own life will matter to him less and less; the faith will become more and more important. The nature of his service will change.

Nevertheless, his faith must continue to be a personal

one; his state of life must not be allowed to stultify it. Consequently, there will be tension. Someone is destined, as priest, to work for the education of youth and is trained for that purpose. He is provided with everything that could be conducive to it: courses, lectures, visiting of schools, conversations with other priests who do the same work. His task is definitively and precisely described; one might expect him to be able to comprehend it once and for all, to know henceforth what is expected of him. But what is exteriorly prescribed must also remain so interiorly alive that his work is constantly stimulated anew by his faith and is able, in its turn, continually to quicken faith, hope and love to new life. And this precisely within his state of life: it should be priestly education conducted by a truly living, believing, hoping and loving priest-educator. The pupil must be able to see that the word of the Lord is at work in living fashion in the heart of his teacher, not only in his private prayer, which may have nothing to do with school or education, but in his whole person, insofar as it is stamped by and serves his state of life. This is true also of him to whom a small and seemingly insignificant work is assigned. An individual may teach geography, for instance, and his schedule may be a light one. Each year he teaches the same material in the same course. As a priest, he might well be discouraged by the narrowness of his assignment. Yet it is precisely as a priest that he performs it. His teaching must somehow bear the mark of his state of life and must radiate the perfect vitality of the divine Word (even though it is only a human word that is spoken). This vitality is his by reason of his choice of a state of life; the state to which his teacher belongs is not insignificant for the pupil.

Similarly, a preacher, whether he is a secular priest or a member of a religious order, must understand that the word is entrusted to him as the representative of a state of life and, within the religious state, of a particular aspect of it. His preaching must not be colorless and monotonous; it must not contribute to a leveling process within the Church by reason of which individual missions lose their distinctive profile. It would be a mistake to regard such colorlessness as a broadening, an improvement or a mitigation. What is important is the distinctive quality that mediates at the connecting point between the indivisible personality of the individual and the indivisible unity of the whole Catholic Church. If one could ignore this distinctive quality, one could also install automatic talking machines capable of teaching all that needed to be known. But the Church lives in her states of life, which, in their turn, contain their particular offices, charisms and missions. In this way, faith, hope and love acquire constantly new profiles that are binding on the member of a state of life or a mission; he receives them in the framework of his state of life as a new talent to be stewarded. His Christian freedom does not consist in subscribing to a spirituality he has arbitrarily chosen for himself. The Holy Spirit does not call someone to the Dominican order only to make him a Franciscan in spirit. One called to a particular order must develop in the spirituality of that order. He should so embody Christian hope, for example, that it develops in him both from the subjective aspect of hope as he understands and accepts it and from the objective aspect of hope as it is represented by his state of life.

It is possible for someone to approach the gift of self full of goodwill and knowing that his chosen state will make new demands upon him. But these demands bear a different aspect when they are actually present, and difficulties arise that he could not have foreseen. Previously, there were certain aspects of faith, hope and love that he had regarded as inalienable because they had helped him find the way to God. Faith, hope and love were most precious to him precisely when they sounded their most personal note. Yet not only are they now to bear the stamp of the state of life as such, but this stamping is actually the responsibility of him who has become the representative of that state. I myself must undertake the assimilation. Its first and perfect prototype is the Son of God, Jesus Christ, perfect man, who as God undertook a mission that he had to accomplish as man; who knew, in the omniscience of God, what he had to accomplish, and as man had to accomplish it in time. Even at the moment when he said: "Father, if it be possible, let this chalice pass from me", he already knew as God what the answer would be; yet he had to accept the chalice as man without the alleviation and the support that his foreknowledge might have brought him. His abandonment by the Father had to be endured even to the deepest darkness. And it is this experience of Christian life, of faith, hope and love, that he also expects of Christians in their states of life. As incarnate God, he is the Bridegroom of the Church. As such, he is also in some way the Bridegroom of the states of life; in his own life, he shares interiorly in their experience and bestows his experience on them. For the Church is a consequence and expression of his Incarnation. She is his body; he has an interior knowledge of the difficulties experienced by man in the Christian states and shares interiorly with him the experience of his own redemptive state as God and man, the difficulties of translating between the divine and the human, both of which are united in his Person. On the one hand, then, the difficulties encountered by the Christian most certainly reflect sin, including original sin—that is, the all too human aspect of man's condition; on the other hand, they also reflect something of the approximation of the human to the divine that was brought about by Christ's free decision to become man and by his perpetually free execution of that decision. The tension between the human and the divine exists prior to their approximation but is seen at its peak in the very moment in which it is overcome and in the manner in which this occurs. Christ is at once the redeeming and the suffering Christ; and he is the former because he is also the latter: he is priest because he is victim, and he is victim because, as priest, he offers himself. And in this tension Christ is God's Word to the world and, in particular, to the Church and her states of life. Whoever lives in one of these states and knows that, through the Church, he is most intimately united with the redemptive life of Christ must constantly realize that God's word is bestowed on him even in the tensions of this life and in the overcoming of them.

***

One who decides to enter the Christian state of life does so out of faith, love and hope. Faith characterizes his basic attitude. It enables him to make his choice in a Christian manner. It is love's task to be the deciding factor in his act of faith, to recognize that God is demanding this, not that, of him and to respond with a Yes. Finally, he hopes, both as a human and as a Christian, that he has found the right way of showing his gratitude to God for his faith and for the life of love that has been granted him.

The character of the three basic virtues is less markedly altered in the married state than in the evangelical state. The external circumstances of one's life, the struggle for existence, the cares and duties of family life create a certain continuity that extends from marriage to death. The married person will seek to live before God the faith he possesses, and his family will necessarily become more and more the arena in which he will exercise his faith, his apostolate. The fact that he is a Christian will leave its mark on the Christian character of his family. Naturally, the married man has some opportunities for apostolic action in the exercise of his profession. Nevertheless, his primary employment is in a secular field; his apostolicity will of necessity have to take second place at work. If he has a certain stability, his faith will suffer no particularly acute vacillations. He will stay on his chosen and traveled path. And he will make the perhaps unexpected discovery that the Christian faith becomes thus the loyal accompaniment, rather than the content, of his earthly life.

Not infrequently, the erotic experience that belongs to human nature plays a decisive role at the time of choice. A man is in love with a young woman or is made uneasy by his desires. Hence he approaches the choice with a certain predetermination. He is not free and unhampered, but somehow bound, even when he is not yet actually betrothed. He makes his choice initially because the young woman is there. Later, when he makes the Spiritual Exercises or recollects himself in some other way in God's presence, he becomes aware that his a priori choice was not a genuinely Christian one, but that his feet are now set on a course blemished by the fact that he did not choose it for purely Christian motives. There is, perhaps, no question of his making another choice, for he has a wife and children. He must try, therefore, to adapt himself to and make the best of his situation. Even this honest assessment of it is something good. For a moment, the full sun of faith breaks through the clouds and illumines the entire landscape. He sees that he is much more dependent than he had expected on God's love. He must hope more strongly that, in spite of everything, God will, by his transforming grace, give our human patchwork the character of something whole.

Certainly a similar situation may occur in the life of a priest or a member of a religious order. Someone may suddenly realize that his choice of a state of life was not based on pure motives. Perhaps it was ruled by ambition, anxiety, love of learning or some other worldly motive. Like the married man, he cannot begin all over again. His life, too, will be somehow divided. But he is, nevertheless, in a far more favorable position than the married man, for he is alone and can dispose of his own life. The grace for a new interior effort will not be lacking to him. Perhaps, by his genuine willingness, he can—like the rich young man in the Gospel—win from God the right to enter upon the way of "leaving all things".

In addition, there is the normal difficulty that arises in the priestly or religious state: that faith becomes institutionalized and regularized, thereby losing its vitality; that between the faith one had when one made one's choice and the faith one has now there yawns an abyss in which charity and hope are more or less buried. As a student, the individual was made acquainted with the meaning of the institution; he learned dogma from this perspective and even worked out scientifically for himself certain areas of Christian truth. Perhaps, by the time his studies had ended, he had become someone who could explain the faith intellectually and defend it with a certain dogmatism, but was far from being able to live a life of love for and hope in God. He falls prey, consequently, to the danger that threatens all who proclaim the word of God: that the word becomes gradually for them a "truth for others". He defends it passionately, but his own soul is not touched by it. He distributes it as though it were an alms without bestowing the gift on himself. Eventually, he becomes aware that he has mastered faith, hope and love as he would master a subject to be taught in school, but that he does not himself live by them. They have no further appeal for him. They are like wares, and he himself like a merchant who seeks to present them in the most attractive way possible. The packaging, which he does himself, can seem more important than the contents. And he notices something else: that he has a tendency to put people into categories, somewhat as a doctor diagnoses illnesses. And he has for every category a remedy that is somehow derived from the word of God; but it is a word that has gradually become no more than a remedy for this or that illness (from which he himself does not suffer). Faith is no longer believed; mankind is no longer loved; everything seems quite hopeless.

It is high time, then, for the word he proclaims to assume once more a central place in his prayer. To possess the word, one must have struggled for it in prayer. One must make it one's own before one can give it to others. Whoever reduces the word of God to the status of wares has become unworthy of his ministry as a servant of Christ. To be worthy, he must give himself to his hearers together with the word—not in a way that will draw their attention to the preacher that proclaims the word, but in a way that will enable God to see, in the proclamation of the word, the grace that is bestowed and accepted by the preacher. The word's passage through the priest or religious must have something dramatic about it so that the word remains living.

Besides the word he preaches from the pulpit, there is also the word he proclaims in his daily life. Even though he had the intention of consecrating his life to the divine truth, this word, too, can gradually evaporate. In religious life, obedience to the rule, the daily schedule and even prayer can lose their substance and become mere formalism. Exteriorly, the individual may appear exemplary in his observance of the rule, and he may even direct all his energy to preserving this facade; but the faith on which the whole structure once rested has become rotten. Even though he is still working on the ornamentation, the foundation is no longer able to bear weight. His memory is well acquainted with the canonical hours and can reproduce them at the right time and with the requisite precision, but they no longer speak to his spirit. And the situation can grow worse: the religious knows exactly what attitude his superior expects of him and what answer he must give to specific questions, and he gives it punctually at the proper time, but his own person remains untouched by them. This de-formation [*Ver-formung*] of life is not far short of the center of his being. His condition is almost hopeless because the person can scarcely react to it any longer. He will have to be practically overwhelmed by grace if he is to find the courage to begin again and let all that has frozen within him begin to thaw.

It often happens that, while still in the world, a particular priest or religious was familiar with the world's temptations against faith, hope and love and could defend against them with corresponding acts of faith, hope and love. Now that he is in the religious or priestly state, these temptations come to him no longer—or at least not predominantly—from the world. They come from within, from the life of faith, hope and love itself. He experiences the usual temptations that beset one who tries to base his life entirely on these fundamental acts: the monotony; the repetition of the same words at prayer, of the same ceremonies, the same feasts; the encounters with the same persons to be loved, with the same truths that should form the hope of his Christian existence. At some point, he has failed to give full weight to being a Christian, and the sickness has spread from there until it threatens to make everything empty and weightless.

There is but one remedy: that those in the evangelical state, like those in every other state, regard faith as something living, as something that daily makes new demands upon our whole life. Day by day, God's love is bestowed on us anew so that we, too, can give it anew to God and neighbor. In new hope we are daily to submit everything to faith—to turn all that we experience, all for which we pray, all that we read, all that we perceive into a nourishment for faith that will nourish it to the extent that we are ready to let ourselves be nourished by faith, that is, by the word of God. Whatever in any state of life is monotonous must become a perpetually fresh adventure through the ever new vitality of this Word that is the Lord himself. For the adventure of God's becoming man remains thrilling for all ages: its vitality is to be not only objectively transmitted to all ages by the Church and her states of life but also lived out as an example in faith. Thus all states of life are obligated to bear the spirit of the Incarnation as the Son of God bore it all his life long: the living Holy Spirit, who causes the wonder of the Father's love to shine through all the monotony of earthly life.

VI

Consequences

For One Making a Choice

One making a choice experiences a number of changes that are conditioned by the choice and are modeled on the series of events that shaped Mary's life, from her meeting with the angel to her dismissal with Saint John the Apostle at the Cross, but also on the Lord's life, from his decision in heaven to redeem mankind to the realization of that decision on the Cross. But for the individual faced with making a choice, the time of most obvious change is the time before his choice, whereas we know almost nothing about the Mother up to the time of her assent and can only make deductions about the Lord's life in heaven by contemplating the Old Testament through the New and considering, in the incarnate Word, the process of his Incarnation and his generation by the Father.

The situation is reversed for one making a choice. If he had to render a faithful account of the history of his soul and its decisions, he would probably have much more to report about the time before his choice than after it. And yet, from the time he makes his choice, his whole being must remain open to the call of God so that he may let himself be conformed to it and may be ever more open to the Lord and the Lord's election of him. Previously his decisions were more or less plausible; they were

determined by his development, by the personal character of his will to surrender, by the inner experiences
that convinced him of the necessity of making a choice,
by the small events that shaped his life outwardly and
had their echo in his spiritual experience. Now everything must be adapted to the Lord's objective election,
which is made known to the individual only indirectly:
as grace, as the hearing of a call, as a quality that the
Son shares with the Father and the Holy Spirit in their
redemptive will for the world. The individual sees himself included, as it were, in the Lord's decision; when he
made his choice, he merely participated in an earlier,
original choice that took place in God and of which he
was himself the object. And what he ought to be, what
God intends him to be, is already exemplified in the Son
and is everywhere evident in him. And despite the great
distance that separates the believer from the Son, he sees
in the Son what he himself has to be; he sees it there in a
perfect and divine way. And he sees, besides, that the
Lord offers himself as a model for imitation. What
seemed, from a distance, to be but one fact among
others—the fact of the Incarnation and earthly life of
Christ—becomes, as we draw closer to it, more and
more comprehensive until it absorbs and completely
embraces our whole life. The convert who recites the
Creed at his entry into the Church confesses his belief in
certain apparently firmly circumscribed truths; these
truths are not simply a norm, however, but are also
simply realization, a reality with which his life cannot
keep pace. The more he immerses himself in the truths of
faith that he has affirmed, the more there will be opened
to him worlds that he can never even survey, let alone
conquer. So it is also with him who chooses. Neither of

them finds the reality of the Lord repulsive because it is perfect and therefore inimitable, because it disappoints and rejects all striving. Rather, in believing and choosing, they find themselves initiated into this reality.

The Son chose to be obedient to the Father even to death. His choice was so perfect that it could be perfectly realized without gap or distance. The believer chooses to follow the Son, the way of service to the Father together with the Son. He knows that the Son followed this way to the end and fulfilled it in every detail; in any case, then, the believer must do nothing that would be incompatible with the Son's way. On the other hand, he will be resolved to do whatever the Son did: to humble himself in service, which is the true meaning of the Incarnation— in service even to death on the Cross, which is the instrument of redemption. The changes the believer contemplates in the life of the Son, from a small child to a mature preacher and to a body hanging on the Cross, he will understand in faith as the expression of Jesus' inner state, of his spiritual decision and its consequences; he will see them as the various stages in the realization of the Son's absolute obedience to the Father. This is the consequence of the Son's choice. One who chooses can gauge thereby what consequences his own choice ought to have. It must not happen that an individual makes his choice and then lets it slip unnoticed into the past. The effects of his choice in his chosen state of life are not his to determine. For him, as for the Son, they are the function of obedience. But this does not mean that the individual should let God do the work while he himself remains but a passive instrument; on the contrary, he must keep before the eyes of his spirit the meaning of the way followed by the Son: the way to the Cross, where redemption takes place, where, in the fiasco of human success, complete divine success is won. The disciple must make his decisions with the Cross in view. For him, too, sacrifice is the ultimate measure of his obedience because the full measure of the Son's obedience was made known by his sacrifice on the Cross. And this meaning of the life of faith is to be manifest not only in the outer circumstances of one's life but also in one's inner disposition. This is difficult for man because he understands best the things he apprehends through his five senses; but in the last analysis, it is the function of the body to express the soul. The fullest expression of inner reality is the Son's abandonment on the Cross.

The time leading to the choice of a state of life is usually the richest in experiences and the most filled with demonstrable events. But this is not the ultimate criterion. We must not forget that the Christian's faithful relationship with the Lord in daily prayer and daily perseverance in his chosen state is more important than every dramatic religious experience. It can happen that the outward stability of a Christian life conceals within itself a mystery of privation: the Lord requires of a person a contribution, a particular strength, and he takes it out of the person's Christian life without the latter's being able to say what is taking place; he knows only the pain of privation. This condition can persist for a long time even though its "outcome" can be summarized in a few words. Something of eternity's stooping over time is visible in it. We are accustomed to look for an end to all we suffer or do or pray. But this other persistent condition is also proper to Christian life and is to be found precisely in one's state of life. To submit so completely to God's action in the soul that one renounces all changes, or, at a certain moment, simply to entrust to God the completion and the outcome, even the process, along with one's ability to recognize the changes that may be wrought, can be the duty and the essence of one's state of life. One perseveres in a kind of open expectation without pressing for a conclusion. Nothing more! This may be the most significant consequence of one's choice of a state of life, for it gives expression to what is, perhaps, the most personal union with the Lord: the entrusting of one's whole being so completely to him that he can do with one precisely what he wants to do, without let or hindrance, but only as he himself wills, even when one senses nothing of what he is doing. And this attitude, which is to be seen as a gate and an entrance, then enables the individual to make an ever greater gift of self—a gift that is stamped less and less with the mark of his own effort in order to receive more and more the features of the Son's gift of himself to the Father.

It is possible to survey everything the Son is and does as man from the point of view of his decision to redeem the world. And we know, too, that throughout the ages he has placed at the service of this decision everything in him that is visible or has remained invisible. But because it is his will to lead men home to the Father, he assigns to those who have chosen him a special place in his work of redemption. He wants to carry them in such a way that he, in turn, is carried by them; his will, which is identified with the will of the Father, wants to make their will so indistinguishably one with itself that his will can eventually appear to be a part of their will, identified with the will of the Father. This is his special way of bridging the distance between God and man: that, in making his choice from all eternity in heaven, he also decided that his choice should embrace our choice. The obvious consequence of this is that we, in our sacrifice and cross, will never be as abandoned as he was, because he has already united us with himself in his abandonment. Hence we can be certain in faith of his presence even when we are not sensibly aware of it. Thus the innermost consequences of our choice are contained and can be found in his choice; and from his choice they act again upon ours.

If I had made no choice but you had done so, I would be unable to understand the effects of your choice upon you. What you do happens, so far as I am concerned, on the basis of something nonexistent, something imagined; I can find no other way of explaining it than to assume that you live in a world of "as if". This assumption is coextensive with my inability to understand. To explain your conduct, you call upon grace. I, who have made no choice, would prefer to explain your whole attitude in another way, perhaps from a purely psychological standpoint. And the more right your choice is for you, the more dedicatedly you live in the state of life you have chosen, the less reasonable or comprehensible will be the effects and changes of your choice for all who do not share the grace of a complete choice. Essential processes always take place in the essential areas of one's state of life. Besides the changes that occur in the empirical life of believers (whether they are aware of them or not), there is also one's whole existence in the Lord and in the Church, the whole objective world of prayer. In respect to prayer, there are certainly characteristics one can identify in the one who prays: his submissiveness and his flexibility. But these characteristics come more and more to bear the imprint of the Lord and to be appropriated by him. There is also the sphere, formed by the

Church's treasury of prayer, where all these relationships meet and have their unconditional reality but are
withdrawn from our grasp. In other words: the more
intimate our relationship with the Lord, the more he
unites us with himself, the more mysterious will be the
effect on us and all that relates to us, the more mysterious
will be also the way in which we are called into service.

Someone believes that God is his Father. He ponders
the care fathers have for their children and how pleased
they are when their children ask them for something
with confidence and gratitude and accept their gifts
without hesitation. And so he prays to God: "Give us
our daily bread." He asks for what he and his family need.
He knows his needs, and his request remains in proportion
to them. Someone else may go further and pray for the
faith of persons with whom he is not even acquainted.
He tries also to pray that the will of God be done in
matters about which he is little informed and that he
need not even put into words. The more a person dis-
tances himself in prayer from his own concepts and
needs, the closer he comes to the region of God. There is
a transcending of one's own concerns that leads one to
the concepts and concerns of God, to his eternal over-
abundance. When two people are united in an egotistic
earthly love, it often happens that each wishes for the
other what he wishes for himself. His wishes have, at the
very least, some reference to himself: "I wish you had a
beautiful dress" is practically the equivalent of "I would
like to see you in a beautiful dress." Love must be
considerably greater than this if one is to wish for or
bestow on the other something in which one has no share
oneself. And that is what one should achieve in prayer
and in the proper attitude of service to God. Our state of
life can help us to do so. It transports us into a realm

where we are not in control, into a region where we let God have his good pleasure without consciously wanting to share it at all costs, in the belief that there is a kind of participation of which we need know nothing. Our state of life mediates this participation because we have already placed our whole personality at its service for the life and action that God wills for us, and because this dedication in our chosen state is easily transformed into prayer.

When someone has deliberately neglected to make his choice, it is an indication that he has consciously established and affirmed human limitations. The narrowness of his personality, the narrowness of the relationships in his life as he sees them and can arrange them from his narrow perspective, are satisfactory to him. He does not want to become involved in something transcendent and more than human that might have unforeseeable consequences in his life: in the unsearchable relationship of Father, Son and Holy Spirit. He gets along with the person he is now; this is the way he wants to remain, the way he feels comfortable with himself. He sets limits on earth, with the result that he is limited in heaven as well. The choice, made in truth, gives us an opportunity to transcend our nature once and for all so that we need not wither in it forever. We have this opportunity because God assumed our nature. He came down to us that he might raise us up with himself, and, after one has reached a certain height, one sees nothing more because it is— not heaven precisely, but the influence of heaven upon us. By making our choice we give the Lord the keys that enable him to be active in us in accordance with his choice.

A saint is one who renounces his own efficacy in favor of God's efficacy; but because God never remains in our debt, he gives his divine efficacy back to the saints as though it were their own. If a person chooses to do the will of God, he can do so only because the Son chose to do the will of the Father and because the choice of the believer is assumed into the Son's eternal choice to become man and to redeem the world. This becomes especially clear in the evangelical state: whoever chooses this state chooses, not what is his own, but what belongs to the Son. He renounces his own narrow views and steps, as it were, into the uncertain. But this uncertainty is the truth and certainty of God, which appears uncertain to us only because, on account of our sinfulness, we can no longer be certain of God's certainty and are actually able to see only blindly. Blindly, for our eyes do not see; but seeing, because we share in the Son's vision. Blindly, because we are still human; but seeing, because we have received a share in the triune life. Our blind faith is embedded in the Son's seeing faith, in his vision of the Father. That is why it will never be possible to understand religious life from a natural standpoint.

***

Years after a person has made his choice, the circumstances surrounding it have faded and he himself, who has lived a long time in his state of life, has become mature, he can and ought to look back upon his choice to see the extent to which it has been a determinative factor in his life, how it is related to his state of life, which aspects of it have flourished and which have become stunted. Such an objective evaluation can be most helpful to the individual and can be useful also to others and to his state of life as such. It should be undertaken with no trace of sentimentality or subjectivity. It is not enough merely to decide that one would make the same choice today or that one would have chosen otherwise if one had known what was to come. One must confront the two—the person one was then and the person one is now—in order to see what has happened with the passage of time. What has become of the strength and enthusiasm that then accompanied the choice, and the arguments that supported it? It is possible that the process of maturity, perhaps even of attrition, has gradually brought quite different motives to the fore. However that may be, one who has made his choice sincerely before God and who wanted to do what was most pleasing to God should be able, without too much reflection, to gain some sense of the degree of God's satisfaction with him. Undoubtedly he has been remiss on all too many occasions. The question, however, is whether, along with his remissness, he has also preserved his essential openness, whether he is still fresh enough to begin all over again and to find new avenues of access to God, or whether he is content with having chosen God once and thinks that the one choice has cost him so much that no one can reasonably expect more of him.

An evaluation of this kind is easiest to make in the married state. The decision to marry is often made while one is in love; the question is whether this infatuation was also accompanied by genuine love, whether love has weathered the years, whether married life has been supported by the blessings of faith and prayer, whether God has remained present in the daily life of the married couple, to what extent small worries, the "struggle for existence", have overgrown God's seed. In marriage, it is also easiest to discover where disappointments began and mistakes crept in. The marriage did not fulfill its promise, or the couple did not do so, repeatedly putting off its fulfillment until tomorrow. In making his choice, the married man was determined to lead a fruitful life in God, a life in family, profession and Church that would be responsible before God. How much of this has never come to pass! Perhaps this wife, these children, would have remained closer to God if they had had a different husband and father. When he made his choice, he had an image of himself that was perhaps strongly marked by fantasy. But when he was young he knew that many things about this image could still be changed. Many possibilities were present, though half hidden, and he expected many of them to develop. In ripe old age, on the other hand, he sees that many of the things he had hoped to develop have been neglected; that the image he had then was perhaps not such a false one, but that he did not hold fast enough to it.

Because of the absolute nearness of the sacraments and his constant association with what is holiest, the evaluation will be easy for one who has chosen the priestly state. His judgment will perhaps be harsh, since every failure stands out strongly in the light of the Absolute. The word the priest administers, his prayer, his closeness to Holy Scripture, the sermons he preaches, the instructions he gives, all remind him of what God expects of men and especially of him. If he has grown cold in the service of God, if he has taken his place on the sidelines or has been overwhelmed by the cares of daily living, he will nevertheless have a sense of the distance that separates him from God and, if his environment does not make it wholly impossible, will readily find his way back. He knows that the grace it is his privilege to mediate to others is not denied to him. Only if he were to lose the faith he proclaims to others (and this would be the worst that could befall him), only if he were to read his failure as an indication of how little efficacy the word of God has for him—only then would he have no further confidence in its efficacy in others. This would be the most difficult condition from which to make a new start. Grace would have to work one of its miracles. It is unlikely that he would succeed in returning little by little to the faith. When one is so far away, it no longer seems worth the effort to reconsider something one has already renounced.

The member of a religious order will evaluate the years of religious training during which the ideal that first prompted his choice should have unfolded and developed. He will be aware of much darkening of this ideal; in the worst case, he will have established himself spiritually in a fixed position. If his choice was a right one, however, he should be able to find again the grace that was based in his choice. Cost what it may, that grace must be rediscovered and reintegrated with the idea he now has of his order and his rule. Just as the honest married person knows that the unpleasantnesses of daily life are there to be overcome and to enrich his marriage, even so must the religious understand the obstacles inevitably presented to him by the state of life he has chosen.

All who have made a correct choice will discover that the special joy and the characteristic inner plasticity that accompanied the choice cannot last in the same way forever. Nevertheless, they will experience, with regard to their choice, a great peace, a peace such as they have never before experienced and that is proper to the right way. Irritations, disappointments and sorrows of all kinds will not be lacking to them. But there will also be the certainty that they are on the right road. This certainty will help them grow to maturity; it will manifest itself in a grace that can be transmitted to others. There are some things one can give to others only when they have become truths in oneself.

For One's Surroundings

When the Son begins his public life, he is in full possession of the Father's teaching. But his obedience so binds him to the Father that he is nevertheless constantly engaged in searching for and seeking to know the will of the Father. He excludes nothing; he is ready to accede to this will in whatever form he may encounter it. He does not want to treat the Father's teaching as though it were something ready-made in God and entrusted to him for proclamation. He does not want to act toward it with a kind of arbitrariness and superiority as though it were impossible for the Father to reveal his truth in an even greater form and to make his will known to the Son in a way the Son cannot conceive of as man. The Son stands before the Father ready for every change and adaptation, and this without detriment to his property of being himself the Word of the Father. He remains submissive to both the familiar and anticipated and to the perpetually revealed will of the Father, striving to fulfill but not to anticipate it. He remains in adoration.

Then come the first results of his preaching: his first disciples. They are so important to him that he not only behaves toward them as a teacher does toward his pupils but even condescends to be himself the milieu in which they live. He adapts his divine word to their understanding and takes images and concepts from their milieu, which he builds into the new milieu he has fashioned for them. In this way he mediates in both directions: from mankind to the Father and from the Father to mankind. For men, he is not only Master but also steward of the truth of life, possessor of the state of life into which they have entered as his disciples, living tradition. In the Son's state of life and in his consciousness of being in that state before the Father and before men are rooted every ecclesial state and consciousness of state. Consequently, the representatives of a state of life must behave toward those who are new to that state as the Lord behaved toward his disciples.

It is not a matter of indifference to the Lord whether he walks alone or with his first disciples. Previously he had spent his days alone in the Father's presence; now man shares the gaze he turns to the Father. This is a change not only for the disciples but for the Lord. He represents for them now the Christian state of belief in the Father on earth. He must settle them in this state, and they, in turn, acquire thereby the right to accompany him and, in the measure of their understanding, to do so as persons who walk interiorly with him in knowledge, comprehension and faith. In practice, this means that the state must pay attention to its members and must introduce newcomers to their new way of life. If the Lord allowed the populating of his own world, opening it to the Father and the world of man, it follows that each ecclesial state must do as he did. The Lord does not do all things through his divinity. If men are to understand his divinity, he must deal with them in human fashion, must translate and make accessible to them his absolute truth. Something similar is true also of each state of life. One must give constant consideration to the aspirants who present themselves, yet without sacrificing the absoluteness of Christian truth: a religious order, for example, must, like the Lord himself, adhere to an immutable supernatural rule and must also see to it that this rule is comprehensible and attractive to young people. Something analogous occurs in the married state, though the signs are different. In the religious life, the holy rule is the permanent element; the novices are the new element to be introduced. In marriage, the human institution is the permanent element; the spirit turned to God is, in each instance, the new element to be taken into consideration. It is self-evident that in marriage a living encounter occurs on the human level. But it is often hard to find in marriage the place where it is embedded in living fashion in the milieu of the Church. This milieu, moreover, as well as married persons in the Church and the Church as a whole, must constantly strive to interpret God's teaching for married persons, to have an interior understanding of their life, and, on the basis of this understanding, to bring about a twofold adaptation: the adaptation of ecclesial truth to conditions in the lives of married persons and the adaptation of their human truth to conditions in the life of the Church.

A state of life is a place of service, and such a place must be in every way suited for service, and, in regard to serving God, for the demands God will make on those who serve him. For God's requirements are unquestionably absolute, a fact most clearly expressed in the Son's absolute gift of himself on the Cross for the salvation of the world. The Son's state before the Father is characterized by the fact that the Son always takes his place where the wishes of the triune God can best be accomplished. In this twofold relation—his readiness to serve God and his establishing a relationship to the world to be redeemed—the Son establishes the Christian state of life. The first state he establishes is that of Christ: the state of the man who is also God. As God he understands what God needs; as man he understands what man needs. But because he is both God and man, he also understands, as man, what God needs, and what God needs always refers to man who has alienated himself from God and must be brought back to him. The translation of the divine into the human in such a way that man will no longer be far away from God, but near to him, this translation that Christ takes upon himself as mediator, is therefore itself a part of the redemption and a fulfillment of the need of the Father and the neediness of man. The mediator is like a simple equation from which items entered on both sides can be removed. By his service he becomes the meeting place of all that takes place between heaven and earth. He is this meeting place as a living, free person: he regards nothing as already established, as mechanical or habitual. The Father, too, remains free in the sending of the free Son, and man also remains free: an offer is made him and he is free to decide what he will do about it. This freedom of the God-Man to be and to act is the foundation of the ecclesial state and the world out of which a state of life is able to become a new milieu. The ecclesial state is the possibility, established by the founder of the Church, of letting Christ's state continue to exist and of giving human existence on earth the opportunity to live with this state of Christ as its milieu.

That is why it is important for the Church to be concerned not only for individuals but also for the states of life. People are more apt to be concerned about individual marriages than about the married state as such. But there is need to structure the state of life in such a way that both those who belong to it and the Church as a whole will more easily encounter in it the will of God. It is perhaps in the religious state that one is best able to detect this spirit of the state as a whole.

A state of life is a living expression of the fact that we must unite ourselves with the service rendered by Christ, which was always an adaptation both to the will of the Father and to the needs of man. The forms of the various states of life bequeathed to us by the Lord cry out to be filled with his spirit. They are the dwelling he has left behind and in which we, his heirs, are permitted to live, but always with reverence for his spirit, which fills the house as vitally now as ever before and which is more than able to incorporate our service in choice and state of life into his eternal service in the presence of the Father.

***

One who has made the right choice and has actively persevered in it cannot fail to act as a blessing on his surroundings. This blessing does not have to be as out-wardly tangible as a young mother's joy in her children or that of a novice master in his novices. It is something lasting and peaceful that itself emanates peace, certainty and joy, and causes them to shine on all about it. The life that has been chosen has proven to be a good one. Through all difficulties and sorrows, the married woman has stayed at her husband's side. Love has been able to withstand all disappointments and dangers. The right-ness of one's choice is never shown by the absence of troubles, but rather by the fact that life stands the test in them. The state of life bestows genuine life and guarantees God's grace to all who abide by its law.

If the choice brings peace, it will become an experience through which others, too, may grow to maturity. Certainly each one must find his own way. But precisely in what relates to one's decision and choice, there is a great advantage in having come upon right decisions and their consequences along one's path of life. Hence no one really knows how far his apostolate extends by the simple fact of his having made the right choice. But the joy of this thought must not make the person who has chosen forget that choice is, in the first place, a grace from the God who made the first choice and, in the second place, the obedience of a free human individual, and that, in consequence, neither party can impose it on others as a model. It may be offered to others as an example, but freedom of choice must be allowed both God and man. This is true even in the case of a close relative, perhaps of a son who is about to make his choice, or of an individual who would like to enter the religious order to which one belongs and who asks one's advice. Like a seed, a right choice has the ability to become fruitful in others in two ways: as a choice per se and as a right choice. Often it is enough for others simply to see the life of one who has made his choice: it speaks for itself and has no need of further recommendation.

By the maturity and peace he has won, one who has remained true to his choice in the religious life can be of great help to the individual who has become uncertain or alienated. He will have faced the same or similar problems, but he has been able to master them and can share his experience with one who is still searching for answers. He can pray for him and present his own life so plainly to him that his brother will find strength and security without need for words. In addition, he who has chosen rightly will be able to influence the whole state of life to which he belongs. The exemplary lives of certain members of a religious community, whether superiors or brothers, their peace and steadfastness, their fidelity and reliability, raise the level of the whole state by inspiring confidence in its power as a form. It is not only the individual's virtue that shines forth but also the living significance of the rule he observes and has incorporated into his life. He lives harmoniously in a house of his order; he has not worked out a private existence for himself in some isolated corner of it. One can learn from him what life in this particular state really is and how superior it is to the alienation and insecurity of those who have either made no choice or have been unwilling to adapt themselves to the laws of the state they have chosen. When the true religious faces some difficulty, he finds such support in his choice and his rule that he can spare himself every personal problem; the difficulty is resolved quite simply. And all goes well with him. There is a great saving of strength in religious life. One does not have to stamp one's personal question mark on every event. When one is transferred to a new place and undertakes a new assignment, one does not have to ask how suitable this is for "me", how "I" will measure up with "my" abilities, and so forth. For him who has given and dedicated himself to the Lord in a particular state of life, all is provided.

It is true of every state that members of the same state have much in common that can keep them alive. A true priest, filled with love, loyal to his duty and full of reverence for the mysteries he is privileged to administer, is for all his colleagues a living witness of the fact that such service is possible even for a lifetime and that no one who occupies himself with the holy things of the Church need ever come to grief as a result. Perhaps it is easiest for the priest and religious to imitate the happy members of their state and to be nourished by their good example because the objective sources from which they draw their stability are the same for all. Good marriages should be able to demonstrate far and wide the sanctity of marriage; this should be all the more true of priests and religious. Most people strive for the natural goals of marriage. Others are more attracted to the two states rooted in the supernatural, for which they feel a special affinity although they are not certain that their natural drives and inclinations will permit them to follow this path. The obstacles are of a more spiritual nature than in the case of marriage. One can find help here in the example of persons who are balanced and happy in their priestly or religious lives, who do not appear to have exhausted all their strength in the struggle against their lower nature, but who have been freed by their continent existence for a life of love.

For the Church

It is not by chance that the Church is called the Bride of the Lord. She is such because she is our mother: even more fundamentally, because the Son has assumed toward her the role of Bridegroom and by his gift of self has brought about that of his partner, his Bride. The fact that the Church is Bride is a lasting proof of the Son's living love. "Bride" is a concept that receives its life from the concept "bridegroom". It is the Lord's will, then, that the Church possess a vitality such as he himself possessed on earth as man. As Bridegroom, he has poured so much life into the Church that this life endures without diminution throughout the ages. If the Church should cease to be Bride, it would be a sign that she had ceased to participate in the Lord's living nature.

The Lord invites us to be the Church, to enter into her as living members: to live her life and to give her a share in our life. His redemptive will takes effect in such a way that those to be redeemed are not only its objects but also cooperate in it. Everyone who makes his choice in the name of the Lord brings into his life something of the Lord's life and, by his choice, assures the Lord of a good kingdom on earth. Thus the choice quickens the Church in the way the Lord expects. Life is bestowed on the Church not only directly by the Lord but also by the faithful, who, by their free decision, consecrate their lives to the Lord and so take the spirit of bridehood, the spirit of the Church, as the spirit of their lives.

The Church must be solicitous about her own spirit in the states of life. She may not only distribute life through the sacraments; she may also receive it, and, in receiving it, get it back again. In this she resembles parents who, having begotten and educated a child, receive from the child a dynamic new spirit for their marriage—a spirit that manifests itself later, perhaps, in the begetting of more children, but even more, in the fact that, having experienced the stimulus and living impulses they received from the child, the parents let these redound to the child's own good. Parental duties should not be confined to a juridically determined minimum but should be an abundant, freely flowing life. The Church must manifest to the children she has borne the same twofold vitality that Christ manifested to the Father and to man: receiving and giving. The Church receives from God the strength and the predisposition to bring forth children and to bestow on them the faith that comes from God; but precisely because she can do this, she must let herself receive new life from these children. A church whose only concern was to open new fields of missionary endeavor, but that expected no new life from these fields or from the nations and individuals who inhabit them, would fail in her mission to be the Bride of Christ. The Church's fruitfulness and its consequent effectiveness are inseparable from the bridal relationship. In coming into the Church, the Chinese, for example, bring to her something new that inevitably exerts an influence upon her. And the only way the Church can respond to these new impulses is with new life; this is the sign that she has really received them.

The Church, then, must extend her concern to all states of life, including the married state. She cannot give all her attention to the other states, for she has the duty to remain until the Bridegroom comes again and to provide for a certain equalization of the states of life. It is not desirable that all zealous Christians should enter the state of the counsels while only the average or indifferent ones enter the married state. The states live in great measure from mutual exchange, and this is possible only when both sides live a vigorous life of faith. Moreover, it is the duty of those in the priestly and religious states by reason of their state of life to provide, by prayer, sacrifice and the preaching of the word, for the vitality of the faith in the people as a whole and especially in families. Priests

administer the sacraments, all of which should be dis-
pensed; there should also be a healthy balance in the
number of those who receive the sacraments that pertain
to particular states of life. The priesthood exists for the
people, but the family, in its turn, must be receptive
toward the supernatural states of life.

***

The distinctions among the states of life confer on the
Church a certain tension that is necessary for her life and
that, as long as it proceeds from the vitality of the
Church, makes a substantial contribution to the fruitfulness of the Bride of Christ. It is obvious to anyone who
observes the Church that the condition of the Church as
a whole is essentially dependent on the condition of the
secular and religious priesthood. This does not mean that
the Church as a whole is simply at the mercy of the weal
and woe of the priestly state. It does mean, however,
that where there are good priests, segments and centers
of ecclesial life will arise that will have a more or less
intensive influence on the whole Church, but that will,
nevertheless, maintain their vitality only if they soon
combine with other living centers (since they are not
infinite in their ability to communicate). In the collective
efficacy of the personal choice of a state of life, there lies a
certain strength that is communicable to the Church and
that, long before it has had its full effect in the life of a
given individual, is perceptible in the life of the Church,
perhaps as the fruit of the gift by which the Church
enabled that individual to make his choice in the first
place, but also in the way in which the choice is received
and fostered in the ecclesial realm so that it can fruitfully

unfold there. The Church models herself here on Mary in her reception of the seed of God that was bestowed on her by the Holy Spirit. The Church receives the seed of the grace-filled decision that is made in her and, after a certain time, observes that the fruit is developing—a process in which the Church has already had a share. This fruition is, of course, not a physiological process: it is a supernatural seed that the Church has to receive, protect, shelter and nurture. By his choice, the individual plants the seed in the Church. But the Church, which is a community of many persons held together by a common life that finds its expression in the states of life, consistently orders the living impulse that comes to her from the individual in terms of the ecclesial states of life. The seed fulfills its purpose in the state proper to it and, consequently, in the interrelationship of the states. If the priesthood should fail to fulfill its function in one area of the Church, it would not be long before the married state would follow its example. For each state is, in its own way—a perpetually new way—the bearer of the Word that is the Lord. The mystery of the Incarnation forms the lasting and indefectible core both of the Church as a whole and of the individual states: the divine Word becomes flesh. The Christian doctrine receives ever new, living realization in the states of life.

The mother who bears a child knows it is not enough to bring the child into the world; he must be nourished, cared for, educated. This is obvious enough in marriage where it is a question of the physical begetting and raising of children. Years later, the parents can look on the children as their fruit, and everyone understands what an enormous amount of work and care the child has cost his parents. But their marriage is not wholly identi-

fiable with the child; it is also a vital family community
that must be kept vital. There is the relationship of the
parents to the children, of the parents to one another, of
families to other families and to the Church as a whole.
There is a give-and-take between the families and the
Church that is, in its turn, dependent on the give-and-
take between the Church and the other states of life. And
suddenly it appears that the community of the Church is,
as it were, a larger family. The Church herself is the
mother whose children are the individual states of life,
and she must care for them as a mother cares for her
children so that the word can live in them: in the individual state as well as in the relationship of the states to
one another and in the Church as a whole, which lives in
her states of life.

The word has been entrusted in a precise form to each
state of life. There are particular words of the Lord and of
Holy Scripture that are especially appropriate to this or
that state, and the state must see to it that these words
retain their living validity in the Church: words about
parents and children, words about priests, words about
those who leave all things and follow the Lord. Everyone should keep the words that are entrusted, like a seed
or a child, to his state of life. And, in each state, each one
must comprehend the word that is meant for him in
particular and, through this word that is most meaningful for him, should comprehend the other, less meaningful words because ultimately all words apply to every
person, just as each state is catholic.

The whole Christ is wholly God and wholly man, and
everything he does is whole. Whether he prays or works
or preaches or suffers, he never fragments himself and
never loses his powers. He does everything in a way the

Father can accept. Thus the Christian in his state of life must always hear the whole word of God, must be concerned for the whole Church, must always do everything that is expected of him in the life and work that have been decreed for him in a way that is acceptable to God. There is no specialization that excuses him from wholeness. No one can proclaim what only others, but not he himself, hold to be true; no one can preach what he lets others, not himself, put into practice. The whole word is to be borne by all. This is already implicit in the wholeness of the decision about a state of life.

From the Church as an institution, life flows through the states of life to the individual and back again from the individual through the states of life to the Church. Neither of these movements may be replaced by the other. They need each other so that the Church as a whole may remain alive.

The Choice Not Made

If we consider the question of choice from the perspective of the Church's claim on the living states of life, we see that the Church must be concerned, for her own sake, that the faithful find their proper place in life. The hindering or omission of a decision regarding one's state of life cannot but have its effect on the Church: positions that should be filled remain empty, and there is a dearth of individuals ready, within the structure of the Church, to serve the interests of the Church and of the Lord. The living harmony among the states of life and within each separate state is disturbed and suffers. Not only will the individual who has refused to make the decision required of him have a bad conscience and, because he has failed in his responsibility, be burdened with an untruth of which he is unable to free himself, but there will also be a vacuum in the state of life to which he was called. A religious order, for instance, will no longer be able to send the right person to the right place; a diocese will experience difficulties because of a shortage of priests. A plan made in heaven will be thwarted on earth. If Christians could know the number of forfeited decisions there are in the Church, they would be less incensed about many of the things that take place in her. The reason why a particular man occupies a position for which he is obviously unfitted is perhaps that another, better prepared, man refused to do the will of God. Nor is it true that one who seems gifted in a religious way and somehow suitable for any position can fill a given post as well as another and can, therefore, appropriate the choice to himself. One who should have become a priest will not, if he refuses to do so, inevitably become an ideal married man. He cannot claim to be in the place God wants him to be. Because human beings are always looking for ways to escape responsibility, however, they constantly devise new reasons for doubting the actual necessity of a choice and, in particular cases, for justifying their failure to make such a choice. It is impossible to estimate the number of those who have fallen into error through these tactics.

Some persons admit openly that, in their youth, they thought they had been called and felt themselves obliged to make some choice. They were struck by something they read in Scripture or heard in a homily or experienced in prayer. But that was long ago. Today they have lost contact with that event and remember it only "psychologically". They no longer realize that the word of God was offered them then in a particular form, that they could have accepted it and guarded it, that the attraction they felt then was the beginning of an obligation and that, by avoiding it, they lost something essential in the truth of the word. The word did not become flesh in their lives in the way it was intended to do. Something awkward thereby entered into their relationship with the word, often to the extent that they completely abandoned all contact with it. They claim that it no longer speaks to them. They stand in a place where they no longer hear it. Their receptivity has been lost.

However different the ways in which the word of God makes itself known, they all have one thing in common: the word of God is encountered and recognized in them. But the nature of the encounter, the meeting of word and faith, is determined by the word. It wants to be heard where it speaks. Then the hearer has the opportunity of understanding what it has to say to him. It is not permissible to call the meeting place determined by the word inconvenient and to advance a counter-suggestion. The word offers itself in a variety of life situations, but always in such a way that the hearing of the word demands obedience from man. The word is not narrow; it does not restrict man. It always enlarges his horizon; it makes him free and lets him remain so. It even bestows on him the freedom to reject it. But he who makes use of this last freedom must be prepared to be cut off from the word. It may be that an opportunity will be given him later to revise all that has gone before. But an assent in a prayer of decision, the conversion of one's whole soul to the will of God, are not things to be met with on every street corner.

If one who has turned away from God hears the word of the Lord addressed to him, it has little meaning for him. It is otherwise with him who seeks, desires and prays for enlightenment. If the latter comes across a particular passage of Holy Scripture, it is illumined for him with unimaginable fullness—the always unique fullness of the word of God as it offers itself to man. This ever new uniqueness has its permanency in the fact that the hearer accepts the word, heeds it and, in obedience, lives in such a way that he is bound by even the smallest word in which he recognizes the Lord's presence, and is drawn from this first bond into an ever deeper and more total bond. But if he has become alienated from the Lord, the word will be alien to him. If he has destroyed his powers of attraction, he must not be surprised if he is no longer attracted.

VII

Vocation in the Gospel

When the Lord needs apostles, he calls them. Or he has them brought to him by someone he has already called. The matter is conducted with the greatest simplicity and simplification. The Master calls and the disciple answers, and does so in such a way that we know the answer was already contained in the call. The hearer does not need a long time to consider the call; he has only to follow it. The simplest form of answer is available to him: the immediate gift of himself, to which the Lord extends a corresponding acceptance. The call, then, is to be found in the Lord's word to the individual.

We who meditate on the gospel today should place ourselves back into the simplicity of the original meeting and accept the Lord's word the way he spoke it. None of the Apostles requested time to think how he would answer. Those who did make such a request, who wanted first to bury their father or to take leave of their family, were excluded from the Lord's company. The rich young man foundered on the concept of poverty. The Lord did not describe the life that awaited those who followed him. It was a question simply of discipleship, of a community of life with him, not according to some foreordained and foreknown plan. The whole program was the Lord: his life, his Person, his obedience. When the Lord calls, he puts all that he is into his word. In this way, one's certainty of having been called is so great that one need worry about nothing else but one's discipleship.

This means that the Lord affords us even today a genuine possibility of answering him: of reading, contemplating and perceiving his word in such a way that we receive his call in prayer and afterward, in following him, discover why and to what we have been called. Through our acceptance of the call, we receive the further possibility of understanding his word ever more deeply. By their association with the Lord, the disciples grew into his teaching. He instructed them with great care; he surprised them in their foolish conversations, taught and encouraged them. He gave them nourishment so substantial that they were able to live by it and were recognized as his disciples: "Are you not one of those who were with him?" There was a sense of belonging between him and them and between them and him that was far deeper than that between teacher and pupil. It was a most intimate community of life. People knew who he was and what he proclaimed; by the same token, they knew also who his companions were. He did not make himself a part of their lives; he made them a part of his own. This means that we must give ourselves to the Lord if we want to assure the reciprocity of our relationship with him. There is a stability and certainty in the two poles of the relationship. We can think of the Apostles only in the position of those who have been called. That identifies them: they are those who have been called. All their bungling does not change this fact. For it is clear that they belong always to the Lord, that they have preserved the freshness of their call even when they seem to dissociate themselves from it, as Peter did when he vowed that he did not know Christ—although

he wept bitterly soon afterward. Hence they allow themselves to be counseled and do not doubt for an instant
that the Lord is right. Their attitude is always that of
those who know that he is the Master.

With us, the call is always in danger of being relegated
to the past. We rest in it instead of growing in it, instead
of clinging to the Lord day after day in his word, in his
Eucharist and in every other mode of his presence among
and for us. We should attach much more importance to
the call and its duration. We are ready to believe that the
Lord looks down on us from heaven and is present to us
in the Host. But we are less ready to believe that, once his
call has been heard and answered, it continues to echo in
our lives, that it never ceases to do so, that the word must
never become a resting-place. The call should be as
important to us as the most serious concerns of the
Church—both our own call and that of others. We must
remain, at any cost, in the number of those who keep the
call alive in themselves, and we must pray for the grace
to do so. Often we feel that we are safe as long as we
pray. "As long as I pray the breviary every day, as long
as I pray at all, everything will somehow be all right."
But we forget that the call is just as important in our lives
as prayer is. Actually, we should hear again in every
prayer the words: "You follow me."

In instructing his disciples, the Lord said many things
to them that have much relevance for us and can become
rules of conduct for us. He does not spare them; on each
occasion he gives them the whole burden with which
they must come to terms. "This is a hard saying." "Let
him understand it who can." We see from this that the
Lord accommodates his teaching as little as possible to
mankind, so that those who follow him will not have the

impression that they are equal to it. No Christian—
certainly no Apostle—can ever be equal to the Lord's
teaching. All they could do was leave everything to him
and follow him as well as they were able, accepting the
whole burden of his words in the certainty that even
what was difficult, incomprehensible or alienating in
them was rightfully there, since it came from the Lord.
The Apostles had the certainty of those who trust in the
Lord. He, in his turn, kept his eye on them; even when
he ascended into heaven, he did not abandon them, but
sent them his Spirit and remained united with them
forever in the full responsibility he had assumed for
them. They did not need, therefore, to stop at the
boundary of what is or is not possible, for their path
led them deeper and deeper into the never-ceasing responsibility of the Lord. When one person leads another
by the hand, it is never quite clear whether the first draws
the other after him, or whether the second simply yields
and lets himself be drawn along. And the whole security
of the one who is led lies in the fact that his hand is held
by the one who leads him. Yet the leader does not carry
his companion—over difficult mountain passes, for instance; he offers him his hand in the expectation that the
other will do his part. If the latter does not make the leap
himself, he will never cross the crevasse in safety. When
someone like Paul becomes a convert, he makes the
greatest effort thereafter to do all he is supposed to do. It
is not a question simply of grace and merit. It is really a
case of "being led by the hand": doing exactly what the
leader does, but in following him, by virtue of this
following. The leader can move without difficulty; he
who is led imitates the leader as well as he can, but he
moves only because the leader moves. He can never

claim (even as merit on his part) that he has conquered the mountain. He was led up it. He can share the enjoyment of the view. But he cannot equate himself with the leader. The result of all this is a more complete surrender. If the Lord invites us to travel with him, he knows what he expects to accomplish thereby. We do not need to ask: Will we be able to do it? How hard is the way? The leader tells us what we need to know. He does not anticipate the details. One who enters upon the state of the counsels does not have to engage in endless inquiries about the order he will enter. The essential thing is that he serve the Lord. It is astounding how few details the Lord told the Apostles about the way. That is possible only because he knows who he is, and because he knows that he is willing to bear the responsibility for what his disciples do not understand, or at least not yet. Nor has this willingness, this knowledge, become less in the Lord.

VIII

The Vocation of the Lord

As a man the Son fulfills his divine mission: not only in the manner in which, as the eternal Son, he received it from the Father but also in the manner in which, as finite man, he receives it at all times from the Father. He chooses this human form not only to show the Father that it is possible for man to fulfill God's will perfectly but also to demonstrate to man the possibility of fulfilling this vocation. Under these two aspects, which he will pass on to the states of life, especially the evangelical state, the Son lives perfectly his vocation, his service to the Father. His service is a service for the Father and in the Father, and the Father is also its goal. His will is recognized by the Son as the Son's own will. The Father guides the whole course of the Son's vocation. He bestows everything on him but also takes everything from him that seems good to him. If we contemplate the Son from the standpoint of vocation, we might say that the Father is his superior, who has all authority and leads the Son in strictest obedience. Nevertheless, the Son does not have to draw, as it were, on his divine reserves in order to obey; he obeys in all simplicity as man, just as a child obeys his human father. But he relies on his infinite wisdom and omniscience for the second aspect: the translation of his obedience into a doctrine comprehensible to man. As incarnate God, he is the representative of an ever greater doctrine. He reveals himself in his vocation and becomes the Master. He lets himself be, as it were, projected as man in order to make what he experiences and possesses before the Father the content of a doctrine. In much the same way, a teacher, even though he has mastered all the material he must convey to his pupils, nevertheless begins with the easiest lessons. At the moment he may seem to them to know only what he is presently teaching. He is doing what his pupils' lack of knowledge requires of him. He makes no use of his greater knowledge; at most, his pupils may, perhaps, catch a glimmer of it in the background. But the lower grades do not yet know what the upper grades have to learn. So it is with the Lord in his vocation. He makes do with what men deem necessary for the exercise of his vocation although he possesses in the background all the divine resources that are proper to him as God. As he lives his vocation, these resources are, as it were, the deposit of that which is ever greater, which is not yet topical and fruitful for man. For the Son lives a vocation that he will pass on to others after he has lived it himself. When he says that his time has not yet come and that the Father alone knows the day and the hour, it appears to be a kind of limitation in the Son. But this limitation has to do with the form: the form he is molding in order to confer it later upon his disciples and upon all Christians to come. He not only shows the Father that his creation is good; he also shows man that the vocation of service is possible. And he tests it himself. He tests it publicly, explaining it, but as man, not as God. When trapeze artists perform, they usually take some precautions: they stretch a net to catch them should they fall. Nor does the Lord expect his disciples to manage without precautions. Yet he himself lived with the minimum of such precautions that is possible for man, and with these he built safeguards for his disciples. But these safeguards are to be found only on the path of discipleship, which is fraught with risk and extreme uncertainty. He has no place to lay his head. The fact that his Mother could find no room in which to bring forth her Son is only the beginning. His way leads to the unknown, to increasing threats from enemies and ultimately to the inexorability of the Cross.

In this uncertainty he is free to adapt himself to every situation, and in doing so he never forgets his mission. He shows his disciples what it means to live in the "state of the counsels", for what he counsels is simply what he does himself. He renounces everything that might weaken his determination to live and proclaim the will of the Father in accordance with that will and with his mission from the Father. He exemplifies in himself the life of the counsels in such a way that others can share in it and can discern in the renunciation it demands of him and of them, not some pious nonsense, but the expression of his obedience to the Father. And he does this in a completely human way. He adapts himself to human nature as the Father created it. He sleeps, eats and drinks, enjoys good companionship and celebrates festivals, but always with an attitude of pure service and with no estrangement from the Father even at times of relaxation. In all this he is, moreover, completely natural. In the strictest obedience, he is totally autonomous.

He always lets the Father know what he is doing. When he says, "Not my will but thine be done", he reveals his interior disposition to the Father exactly as it is: his thoughts, his feelings, his aspirations. He lays his heart bare before him. His doing so is an act of obedience. On the other hand, he does not accept the Father's will as one accepts the burden of an inevitable fate, waiting submissively for what may come; on the contrary, he is constantly in search of this will so that he may unite his own with it. He uses his knowledge of the Father to formulate a rule for his life, from which he gathers at every given moment what he is to do. The Father and his will are the rule of life for him as a man in his vocation.

His vocation consists in the great tasks of the apostolate, of which the greatest will be the Cross, but not less in all that we label human contingencies and trivialities. Since he has taken his stand in his vocation, he accepts everything that comes to him in the context of this vocation in order that he may give everything the meaning and complexion of his vocation as God expects him to do. He has been from the beginning the Word of the Father; now it is time for that Word to be uttered in human form. What he himself is from all eternity is now assigned to him as his mission in time. As he is eternally generated by the Father in heaven, so he is called as man to administer, present, interpret and proclaim the eternal Word—that is, to concern himself with it, almost as though he were not himself this Word, as though it must be the fruit of his human striving. The reason for this is that the Son's obedience to the Father is consistently valued more than the fact that he is truly the Word of the Father. In illustration, we might point to the example of Mary, who is betrothed to Joseph and yet is the Bride of the Holy Spirit, or to the example of a bride who actively helps her husband and does not insist on being accorded her rights as bride.

On the basis of this attitude, the Lord decrees, for his

followers, the primacy of vocation: "No one who puts his hand to the plow and looks back is worthy of the kingdom of God." The intimacy of every personal relationship is exploded by the demands of one's vocation: service to one's mission must be the all-embracing concern. Thus the Son, in his earthly vocation, opens the possibility of heavenly intimacy in order to give primacy to the mission of redemption, which is what the Father wishes at this moment. The intimacy remains; it is not forgotten. But this is not the hour for it. The Lord knows, even to the smallest detail, how the hours differ from one another. Their value lies always in the fact that every hour bears the visage that is willed for it by the Father. Wherever the apostolate has the primacy, as was the case during all of the Lord's earthly life, one's life must be dedicated to this apostolate. In the examples mentioned above, there is always a question of sacrificing a personal relationship in favor of an objective duty (the eternal relationship of Begetter and Begotten in heaven, Mary's bridehood, the role of spouse in a family relationship and, finally, the burial of one's father are all personal relationships or the expression of them). Nor should vocation be opposed as "action" to the personal relationship as "contemplation". Contemplation, life in the desert, prayer in darkness or on the Mount of Olives are also parts of one's vocation. They do not interrupt it. The Son's vocation lasted without interruption for his whole lifetime.

Something of this is visible in many of the saints. Saint Thérèse of Lisieux talks about her life only because she sees and recounts it in the light of her vocation. She does not describe it for the sake of description; she wants to make a statement and she uses herself, the substance of her existence, as a means of demonstrating it. She understands herself from the perspective of her vocation. The Son was the first to make himself preeminently and wholly a means of demonstration in order to show the wholeness of his mission, in order to fulfill all prophecies in himself, in order to reveal the divine nature by his humanity and to manifest by his love the necessity of serving and glorifying the Father.

The life of vocation is at once open and closed. The Son, who lives his mission, lives openness. He is an open book. Everyone can see that he removes nothing, conceals nothing, reserves nothing for himself. Everyone can learn from the life of the Master how to overcome this difficulty, how to deal with this situation. But this openness is, at the same time, a closedness as regards his mission. The mission, even when it is divine, always has a definite outline. From the perspective of world history, the Son's way is a narrowly circumscribed one. Few conversions and very little outward success accompany him along the way, and it ends in total failure. Its success lies elsewhere: in the effect his obedience to his vocation will have on future ages. Thus God lets us know that he imparts to vocations a value that transcends the personal life structure of the one called, a value that has supernatural, divine characteristics and a fruitfulness that cannot be estimated or evaluated by the one called. The Son does the will of the Father: that is all that need be said. But it is the Father, not the one sent, who plans and calculates the mission. It is the latter's role to accept gratefully whatever may appear improbable or humanly impossible insofar as it is part of his mission. The Son did not use his human understanding to judge God's redemptive plan from a human perspective. Perhaps that is part of the meaning of his prayer on the Mount of Olives: "Not my will be done." For his will, as a human will, might want to rely on human means and measures. He might perhaps fear that his death on the Cross would deprive him too soon of the possibility of being effective in his earthly mission, deprive him of everything he had planned for carrying out the Father's mission, deprive him even of the trust of the Apostles, deprive him of the faith he had sown with so much toil in the numerous souls who have thereby received something and urgently need a further confirmation of their faith. Humanly speaking, the Cross is a scandal not only for the spectators but also for the crucified and abandoned one himself. Today this scandal is more than ever in evidence, not only for Jews and pagans but also for Christians. How many of them would be ready to admit that, measured by the needs of human culture today, the Cross has lost much of its justification, or that they would certainly have been scandalized if they had lived at the time of the actual Crucifixion, that this way of God has nothing in common with their concept of genteel discretion and respectability.

But Christian vocation takes no notice of these considerations. It has its truth in God. God guides it in his wisdom. And God demands service and himself establishes the form of this service in the mission. The Son shows that this objectivity is the highest form of love. He chose obedience as his vocation because he wanted to show the greatest love for the Father and because he wanted to demonstrate the Father's greatest love to man.

IX

The Vocation of the Apostles

What the Apostles experience is what all who have been called by God should experience: that their mission comes to them directly from the Lord. It is not something foreign to them; the Lord has already lived it as an example to them, and something of the distance between the Lord and them has been eliminated by the transfer of the mission. "As the Father sent me, so I send you." The mission he confers upon them is as fresh and immediate as if he had, at that moment, separated it from his own in precisely the form best suited to each particular individual. Hence each individual's mission bears all the marks of having been designed for him alone, although the marks were actually already present in the Lord's mission. Nor is the appropriateness of a mission for an individual something he can ordain at will; it is something placed there—really almost invisibly—by the Lord himself. He arranges things in the way the Apostles must accept if they are to perform their mission properly. And because contact is immediately established in the process of mission, the Apostles do not have to ask many questions; their answer is already present in their acceptance of their mission, in their Yes to it, in their discipleship and its fulfillment, even before they have had time to come to an understanding of the answers, spiritually or otherwise. Those who ask questions and announce some plans of their own at the moment of mission are, in practice, those who do not accept their mission.

In his bestowal of mission, the Lord lays claim to man in a way that demands his immediate and unconditional discipleship. From this first action, the Lord proceeds to restructure, not the mission, but the Apostle in accordance with the mission. To this end, the Lord trains the Apostle, gives him a share in his insight and instructions and molds him more and more into the form of an Apostle. When the disciples begin to follow him, they have no intimation of what is in store for them. As they live and associate with the Lord present in their midst, they gradually learn what he means, what is important to him, what he expects of them. And all this builds on their initial Yes to the invitation to discipleship; it is the fruit of that seed that was buried in their soul. When they occupy themselves with the Lord's teaching they are dealing with something that has already taken root in them; when they ponder questions of obedience or of ecclesial community, these are not problems that have come to them from without, but problems with which they are actually living. Nor is it especially important whether they ponder them correctly or only attempt to do so, with or without understanding, for both are episodes in their life of discipleship and in their effort to do the Lord's will.

The definitive assent to the Father's will is that made by the Lord. And just as he caused the call to the Apostles to issue from his own assent to the Father, so he bestows on them, from this same assent, the grace to say Yes to his call. Their response is a completely simple, unreflected, almost primitive act that nevertheless decides everything: it is made to the God who is alive in Christ

Jesus, of whom they have a presentiment, an intimation, an experience in him, and in whom they believe and hope through him. Once they have taken the first step, without quite knowing how it has come about, they find themselves on a path that leads them further. They have trust; they surrender themselves without yet having received many proofs. They let themselves be drawn by a deep sense of rightness that is at once human and inspired by faith. They are, in fact, very simple, laconic men, for whom every word, once it is spoken, has meaning. They do not believe that an individual would misuse his own given word, that someone would call "Come!" when there was no reason for coming. But the Lord prepares them ahead of time interiorly for the call. He makes them capable of the answer they must give and that he himself has already given. Nor is it by accident that the first disciples are Jews. The whole promise of the Old Testament dwells in them. It is less an action of the intellect than of the Holy Spirit: a feeling for what is right when at last it comes—expectedly, but nonetheless surprisingly. Today, we can no longer experience this directly as the Apostles did. At most, we can point to similar events in the natural sphere: when we observe hereditary characteristics in ourselves, for instance, or in other persons, and it is suddenly obvious that this trait is a family one. A resemblance, a deep identity, is irrefutably present. Or, from another sphere: the experience on seeing a beautiful picture or hearing great music that there has always existed in us a longing, a kind of expectation of finding something like this someday, although we had no idea how it would come about. Now, however, everything in us exclaims: "This is it!" Fundamentally, the experience of the disciples is based on the antecedent redemption of the Mother of God, on the retroactive (or pre-venient) power of the Lord. This experience is ultimately anchored in the unfathomable mystery of God's salvific will and action. The Son, who promises the Father from all eternity that he will redeem the world, knows beforehand all there is to know about mankind and how it is constituted, including a fore-knowledge of his own short life on earth and the whole area in which he will sow his seed during this time. He knows the Bridegroom and the Bride. From all eternity, then, the conferring of grace has been a function of the whole Trinity. As man, the Son sows his seed on earth, but the soil on which it falls is the concern of heaven.

The Lord's own mission is divine and infinite. Hence it is also inexhaustible. Even to the present time, he is constantly cutting new missions from the stuff of his own mission, which will last to the end of time. Nevertheless, our missions differ in character from those of the Apostles because more faith is required of us than of the Apostles for a full assent to the Lord's call. In their day, the Lord was with them as a man among men; he called them with a human voice; they were addressed in human fashion and had the opportunity of maturing gradually from time to eternity. If they had doubts, they were able to discuss them with the Lord in human speech. When the disciples argued among themselves and strove for the first place, the Lord heard them and was able to correct and advise them on a human level. We, on the other hand, must discover this human element within a living faith. This would be very difficult if it were not, from another point of view, an infinite facilitation, for so many others have received their mission and given their assent before us: not only the Apostles but also the saints, the martyrs, the confessors and the countless numbers of those who have walked the way of the counsels. There are the countless religious orders and congregations that seek to model their interior life today on the community formed by the Lord and his disciples and in which the call, the decision, the entrance, the formation, the trials, the sending and the apostolic work are repeated. It is in this ecclesial framework that the call sounds for us.

Day by day as the Apostles accompany the Lord, they become better able to recognize his divine wisdom, his absolute superiority and, in the end, his behavior in suffering, which more than anything else reveals the presence of God in his life. They perceive his right to make demands upon men in order to give them a mission. They perceive his infinite love and this love's right to form men for love and to demand their total love for God. Thus the Apostles experience immediately the fact that they are privileged to stand in a relationship to the Lord that is analogous to the Lord's relationship to the Father in heaven. They find that they share not only the Lord's life but also his mission. They see that he challenges them to do what he does. Simple human things come first like walking, eating and sleeping with him. Then, in the trial missions, come things related to their mission: they are to preach as he does, to proclaim the kingdom, to lay hands on the sick, to drive out devils as he does. And just as he forms a community between himself and his hearers, so must they do: they are not to form another community but to enter into and enlarge the one he has already formed. He prepares them for this work by explaining to them the meaning of his words and by interpreting for them his parables, the interior meaning of which most of his listeners are unable to understand. He draws them as deeply as he can into his relationship with the Father. And when they lose heart and want to go no further, he draws them into his prayer on the Mount of Olives: he wants them to know how difficult his mission is for him. He wants them to know that, insofar as his mission is concerned, he, too, has someone above him, someone to whom he must submit: "Not my will be done!" (And if they fall asleep, then he or the Holy Spirit will explain everything to them later, for know it they must.) Whatever they are able to understand about the mission of the Son is shown to them. And every new comprehension sinks into their being like a seed that must sprout, like a substance from which they are to be nourished.

From the Lord's conversation with his disciples as well as from his prayer to the Father they learn to understand how present the Father is to him. The Lord's presence to his disciples acquires thereby a new radiance. Everything is rooted in the depth of trinitarian life that overwhelms them. In these depths their mission lies hidden. And they know that it is in these same depths that the Son and his mission lie hidden in the Father. Both missions receive their life from these depths. Their apostolic mission is as vitally and truly supported and authenticated for them by the Son as the Son's is by the Father.

When they are sent out with specific duties to perform and the Lord is no longer directly beside them, the disciples are suddenly aware of the distance there is between him and them. They see how poor their performance is in comparison with his. They understand that they can never be like him. And yet, however ignorant and unskilled they are, the Lord supports them to an incredible degree. He does so not only by correcting their faults but also by putting himself and his whole mission at the side of the disciple who is momentarily in difficulty. The Lord not only supplies what is lacking but, by his wholeness, supports the whole. And the disciple understands that he will never be able to measure the extent to which the Lord actually supports him, for the Lord's mission is divine whereas the disciple's mission is merely derived from it. There is in the Christian mission an unresolvable element that has its situs in the Lord's mission and runs its course there, because the essence of every mission has its source in the Son's responsibility before the Father. However responsible a man may be, he can never comprehend this responsibility. We only know that it exists.

The Apostles are aware of their distance from the Lord less in regard to the human element, the relationship of disciples to Master, than in regard to their mission, the relationship of task to task, because, without understanding it, they experience here something of the Lord's eternal mission, and precisely this is what they are unable to measure. Actually, they experience the distance less as it exists between the sinner and God than as it exists in God the Father between the Son and mankind. What the Apostles accomplish is by no means exhausted in that part of their mission that is comprehensible to them and that they can measure and observe. It lies above all in their mission, at the point where that mission, because it is joined to the Son's mission, loses its comprehensibility for them. They have been incorporated into a work process in which they can hope to achieve a certain dexterity in the tasks assigned to them but can never achieve a comprehensive view of the whole process. They fulfill their roles on earth, but the plan comes from heaven. They are like a laborer who packages small items in a factory. He does his work well, but he does not know the customers for whom the packages are intended and who may be in other lands or on other continents. Perhaps he does not even know the contents of the packages. In much the same way, the Apostles do what is required of them in the here-and-now, as the Lord commands, but leave to him the administration of the whole process.

Each time the disciples return to the Lord from their apostolic journeying, they receive from him both criticism and encouragement. Through both they grow to the maturity required by their mission so that the task assigned them becomes for them a matter of the most personal concern. They understand now that they must give themselves totally even to the most clearly defined task: for instance, preaching to the surrounding villages. It is not a question just of repeating something they have learned; they must place in the balance all that they are. Nor is this effort of theirs a measurable one; it must be performed tentatively, with their gaze fixed on the absolute effort of the Lord. Wherever the Lord makes his appearance, it is always clear that he is the Son of God, the Master of those who follow him; at one and the same time he is the Word and administers it. He is not merely someone striving toward a goal; he is someone who is at every moment what God expects him to be. Consequently, the Apostles must strive to be in their vocation what the Lord's vocation requires them to be.

Vocation is a call from the Lord. The Lord puts

himself into this call. Thus one who receives the call receives the Lord as he is in the vocation. On the other hand, it is also true that the Apostles became something new in their vocation: they became disciples of the Lord, and the Lord dwells among them in order to train them for their discipleship. They had to be attentive to what he communicated to them. For just as the Lord is the image of the Father for us, so they, too, had to become models in the Lord for all whom the Lord would call in future ages. The Lord's fruitfulness consists in his being both the seed and the word of the Father. And in him these two are one. When the Lord bestows his word, he also bestows his seed. The Apostles receive his word as seed. And their fruitfulness will consist in sowing this seed in others. This sowing is the divine answer to their vocation, its attestation. (In this connection, the later celibacy of apostolic ministers is a sign of their acknowledgment of the Lord's word. For just as no man can serve two masters, so must one who will be fruitful choose a kind of sowing to which he can dedicate himself: he must be either physically or spiritually fruitful. And since the Lord gives himself as the seed, this is a sign that he wants spiritual fruitfulness and no other from the apostles of the New Testament.) The word, as the Lord gives it to the Apostles, really bears itself; it bears the divine vitality. This word is not only to be received in a living manner by the Apostles but also to be transmitted in a living manner so that it loses none of its own vitality. After centuries of evangelical activity, it should not be any more alien to or estranged from the Lord than it was when he uttered it on earth. The sacrament of the Eucharist is the guarantee of this perpetual life: here the

Word that is the Son is perpetually flesh among us, and the spiritual seed is perpetually the substantial power of God. Sacrament and word, Eucharist and homily, belong forever together and are together administered by the Apostles and their successors.

X

The Vocation of the Successors
Of the Apostles

By giving the Bride, the Church, the form we know, the Lord guaranteed to men of all ages that there would always be calls and vocations that stemmed from the Lord's mission, as vital as the calling of the Apostles—on the condition that the successors of the Apostles would leave to the word its full meaning, that they would recognize in the word the living Christ and in the call the living call of Christ. Neither in the call itself nor in the vocation that followed it should the word lose its original tone. The word contains in itself the power to take the one called into its service. But if the one called makes it a function of himself, the word loses its strength in him. The call is a function of the Lord, a function of his mission. If it is heard rightly, this characteristic will also be heard: that it is a call for now and for always. And our answer must correspond to this characteristic. To live according to the call means to persevere in it: in meditation on Holy Scripture and in Communion, in daily rounds of question and answer, in a never-ending effort to hear and obey. In the Mass the Word daily becomes flesh and blood; in Holy Scripture are to be found the spiritual tidings of the Word that became man and is man for all time.

Just as there was tension in the lives of the Apostles between their mission and the Lord's by reason of the Lord's presence as man (which, however, was always oriented toward the Ever-More of God), so there is tension also in the lives of the successors of the Apostles. This tension must always remain living. Wherever those who have been given a mission by the Lord are gathered together in religious congregations, their superiors must have the ability so to personify the Lord that their word remains the bearer of the living word of the Lord. Their interpretation of the gospel and the rule must be so transparent that the Lord can manifest himself therein without distortion.

If today the various ecclesial states are attempting to concentrate on one time or one aspect in their imitation of the Lord's life on earth, it should not be forgotten that every period of the Lord's life always and unconditionally incorporates his wholeness and that his human wholeness is always the expression and representation of simple divinity. However a call may be constituted or a vocation ordered to the Church, the first requirement is always that it represent this wholeness. The special vocation of discipleship must always be undertaken with a clear conception of the essential nature of the Lord. Individuals may possess natural talents and gifts that come from God and that God has bestowed on them in view of the call he intends to make and according to a plan known to him alone. But the one called will not order his life according to his own talents and, in doing so, perhaps limit God's greater call; on the contrary, he will order it in terms of the call to the Lord's discipleship. It is possible that one who has difficulties with intellectual work may nevertheless feel himself called to an order that pursues just this kind of work, and that a part of his cross will be to overcome the ensuing difficulties. But the effort he must make should not be an expression of defiance ("Under no circumstances will I become a lay brother!"); it must be required of him by the Lord. The first prerequisite for understanding what is or is not so required is a vital relationship to the word throughout one's whole life. The encounter with the word must be so humble and so living that the one called feels himself simply and truly addressed and knows about the truth of what he has experienced in prayer and about the unconditional demand of God. This knowledge must not be made into the object of a cult, into an inner truth that has meaning only for the initiate. Rather, this inner certainty must always issue from the knowledge of the whole and must be in harmony with it. It presumes in the individual, therefore, an openness to the whole word (which is always also an ecclesial word). And it may happen that the individual will encounter, in this openness, the unexpected and unpredictable. That is the opening wedge that constitutes true contemplation—in this case, of the word as the call to and the starting point of a vocation. Then he who hears the call will remain malleable to the word, and there is a way out of all the dead-end streets of weariness, dullness and dryness.

The Apostles fulfilled their mission in a holiness given them by the Lord, yet still as human beings who had not been antecedently redeemed and who had at their disposal only the grace bestowed on them day by day. They had their failures and imperfections, but the nearness of the Lord was so victorious that they always found their way back to him. However, we must not overlook the fact that those who followed the Lord in succeeding centuries could marshal experiences that the Apostles did not have: experiences of religious orders, experiences of the saints, experiences of the Church as a whole. The Apostles stood in the blinding light of the Son who lived among them and were unable to distinguish clearly many things that were more sharply outlined in the half shadows of a later time. In consequence, a certain fruitful tension arises between the original missions of the Apostles with their as yet undifferentiated wholeness and the missions of their successors with the differentiations created by distance. Those of a later age must expose their mission again and again to the full light of the Apostles' mission so that they may participate anew in the light of its wholeness. But they may also let their particular mission be enriched by the many experiences of mission that have developed throughout the history of the Church. Their position is no less favorable than that of the Apostles.

Every mission stands at a point of transition: it builds on tradition and has the duty of making its own experiences available to succeeding generations. Christ himself, who became man in Mary, had to rely on her experience. He is absolute Wisdom, he is God, but he does not disdain what his Mother can contribute: the gift of her life of vocation between her assent and the birth of her Son, and even between her Immaculate Conception and her meeting with the angel. But the concept of tradition always requires discrimination. Vocation is essentially service of the Lord, of the Church and of humanity as they are today. And despite the element of permanency, many things change in the course of time, not only in humanity but also in the Church. Admittedly, men remain sinners and can be understood under this concept. But the conditions of their existence, the ways of addressing them so as to lead them to God, change with the changing times. One who proclaims the word of Christ must not associate himself and his vocation with a group of persons who are ignorant of the world and consequently never reach the world to which they have dedicated themselves and which they want to address. Even a purely contemplative religious order must have a living knowledge of today's world.

XI

The Vocation of the Saints

The vocation of the saints[1] is on an entirely different plane from the vocation of those called to a religious order because it somehow cuts through everything. It is unified, just as the Lord's vocation was unified, because it has its source in the same unity. But it is subject to pendulum-like vacillations that are not present in other vocations within the Church. In the other vocations, the gift of oneself to the Lord is accompanied by the acceptance of a certain form. But the use of a saint's vocation is left completely to God, so that the vocation may outwardly have a disunifying effect. The priest knows to what ministry he has been assigned. The member of a religious order knows what prayers he must say. But the saint, even when he is a religious, is somehow simultaneously at the center and not at the center. He is at the center because he carries out his religious vocation in holiness; he is not at the center because he is aware of another, deeper center that his knowledge, his intellect, his personal faith, perhaps even his obedience are unable to plumb. It is a center that is hidden in God and that God reveals only to the extent

---

[1] Sanctity, as the term is used here, is to be understood not as a general but as a particular kind of sanctity that God bestows within the Church on chosen individuals who, in some mysterious fashion, open and transcend, without destroying, the Church's structure in the states of life.—Ed.

necessary for fulfilling a mission or perhaps for preparing the ground for a mission yet to come.

It may be that God will use the saint's service for a
clearly defined purpose, in a limited place and, from a
human point of view, even for a limited time. But it can
also happen that he will diffuse its effectiveness from the
beginning, letting it operate in a number of places at once
and thus depriving the saint himself of any clear picture.
During the saint's life on earth, his vocation, which, like
all vocations, has its source in the Lord's own mission,
reflects the omnipresence of his mission rather than the
effect of the holiness required by his state of life. In the
mission of a religious, the comprehensible and the incomprehensible exist side by side, and the assumption is
that the area of the comprehensible should be formed and
shaped by human elements: the rule, obedience, the
customs of the order and, to some extent, the unique
nature of the individual himself. The incomprehensible
surrounds this firm core like a ray of light. It would be
possible for a religious to live on a kind of fluctuating
boundary line where the incomprehensible stood in a
particular relationship to the comprehensible. The better
the religious ordered what was comprehensible, the
better God would be able to let the incomprehensible
take effect. For the saint, the situation is almost completely reversed. The comprehensible is a function of
the incomprehensible, the controlled fruit of the non-
controllable that has been left in God's care. It is even
possible that the controlled fruit will reveal very little
order, very little particular holiness, very little that
differentiates it from what other believers are able to
accomplish in similar circumstances, because all that is
decisive about it has been taken in charge and invisibly
used by God.

In the vocation to religious life, there is a period marked by the call: a time of decision during which the world the person lives in can exert a certain influence on him. He can prepare himself for his decision; in most instances, he will know by the time he reaches his majority to what vocation he is being called. For the saint, there is no such specific time of vocation related to human development. Nor is his environment, even if it is a good and Christian one, allowed to influence him much. There are saints who seem to be called to holiness from their cradles and whose childhood takes place in an atmosphere of complete holiness; others have to experience renunciation, conversion. But, in either case, everything remains open; God's call can summon the individual again and again out of his present state and into a new one. It can summon him from virginity or marriage into the cloister, or from the cloister into the desert. But that is not the special mark of the saint's life: on the contrary.

The call to one of the more common vocations is generally linked to a change of milieu, an alteration, a sharp separation from what has gone before. For the saint, on the other hand, there is seldom a question— except in cases of sudden conversion—of a change of vocation. Usually he has to do God's will in the circumstances in which he finds himself. A call to a specific kind of holiness can develop within his vocation; or it can, of course, lead to a vocation. In general, however, it can be said that a call to holiness that does not take place in early childhood is more likely to require perseverance than change.

One called to the religious life understands by his vocation what he has been called to and consciously strives to accomplish what the call demands of him. The saint, on the other hand, never—or at least very seldom—knows that he has been called to sanctity. He carries out his vocation of holiness with a certain lack of concern, though not, certainly, with a lack of strictness, consistency or asceticism. But everything he does by reason of his vocation and to carry out his vocation is done, to a certain extent, with other ends in view. He leaves wholly in God's care the conduct of his vocation, the choice of conditions regarding it, its use, the service it renders. On the whole, his vocation expresses itself rather as an attitude toward God, as an openness to the workings of God in him, than as a distinctive way of life. God reserves to himself the mystery of the system by which he orders his saints.

The evangelical state summons those called to it to strive for holiness, for Christian perfection. It is the saint's vocation to demonstrate a mode of fulfillment for those who so strive. The two vocations can coincide, but it is not necessary. The rule of a religious order is a holy thing; the founder composed it under the inspiration of the Holy Spirit. But the highest rule of the saint has been formed by God alone in his mystery. It is difficult to say when a man becomes aware that he is directly subject to such an exalted rule. Nevertheless, the saint has this kind of knowledge—which, however, is not the same as an awareness that he is the bearer of a mission to sainthood. It is as if grace and merit coincided in a special way in the saint, with grace somehow taking the initiative, but demanding more merit in return.

Beyond a doubt, the evangelical state has a special relationship to holiness inasmuch as the keeping of the counsels binds man to God. What is distinctive about the vocation to sainthood is rather the immediate following of the Lord than the entrance into an organized form of life. As a state of life, the religious state has a certain static quality, whereas the saint's following of the Lord remains more of a movement, with perfect availability. This would be possible even in the world, and not impossible even in the family, although in family life parts of this availability would be preempted by family ties. The perfect fulfillment of family duties is *in itself* as little indicative of holiness as is the perfect fulfillment of house rules in a religious order; both can be done out of a predilection for exactness in little things. Love for the rule is not unconditionally identifiable with love of God. In religious life, the perfect observance of the rule leads to and is a prerequisite for holiness, but it is not identical with holiness. Full holiness is perfect love.

But no one who strives toward God in any of the ecclesial states of life will venture to claim that he possesses perfect love. Believers are always underway, and they know it. But from his eternal perfection God can, if he will, bestow the gift of perfect love. Such a love can move mountains because it is coextensive with faith. It is a love whose wondrous nature reveals itself in the performance of miracles, a love so unconscious of its own perfection that it is like a window opened onto God's infinite love.